Co

Bible quotes are taken from NIV 1984 and from KJV.

Peace in the Pressure Cooker

By

Patti Davis

peace
— in the —
PRESSURE COOKER

Chapter 1

Your Daddy's Gone

"Your daddy's gone, he's passed away." I received that piece of news from my father's nurse. She called me on my cell phone while I sat in my car at the gas station. Needing a little break, I had left the hospice facility two hours earlier, and now it was around six thirty in the evening. I'd been at the facility since the early morning, and I went home to take in the mail and turn the house lights on. I was on my way back to Daddy's side when the phone rang. Ten days earlier we'd made the decision to place Dad in hospice where he could receive some rest and relief from his pain. I was so disoriented after receiving that phone call that I truly didn't know how to put gas in my car. I just stood there, bewildered.

I collected my thoughts enough to call my daughter, Chrystal, who was at her home a few miles down the road. I had to tell her that her dear Poppy had just passed away. She cried. I told her I was frozen in place right there at the gas station, and I didn't know what to do next. Chrystal told me to gas up the car, drive to my home, and she would be right there to pick me up to take me back to hospice to be with the rest of our family.

My Mom

There had always been tension between my mother and me. The level of tension increased during dad's final months of life. When I placed him in hospice, the fear of her husband dying and leaving her all alone left Mom inconsolable and uncontrollable. She was difficult to be around, and at the time of Dad's death, we hadn't spoken to each other for six days. Mom would be at Dad's bedside during the day, and I would go in the evenings when I knew she had gone home. One afternoon her unrelenting fear and negativity took its toll on my emotions. I was spending some personal time with Dad when Mom came barging into the hospital room, shattering our tranquility. She began making demands on me, starting with "Go to the hospice accounting office to see how much this is costing." My spine straightened. I pushed back on her insensitive behavior and selfish attitude; her expectations and demands had become unreasonable.

For months she had displayed a lack of empathy toward my siblings and me, never acknowledging our feelings or our needs. Instead of focusing on Daddy, she required everyone to focus on her. I had become hardened by her haughty behavior and stood up to her that day. However, no one stands up to Lori Wells, and she began seething with anger toward me.

It was a very sweet time with Dad and my daughter as we spent our final moments with him before hospice removed him from his room. I made phone calls to my sons. These wonderful young men cried for the loss of their grandfather—their hero. My daughter and I spent an hour alone with his body during which we groomed his hair, straightened the bed, and cleaned up the room. I leaned over him one more time to smell the top of his head and tell him goodbye.

My heart was calm and full of comfort knowing that dad had accepted Christ into his life just a few weeks earlier. I knew his pain was gone, and for the first time in his life he felt peace. I had carried the burden of my parents' souls for thirty plus years.

And in the weeks to come, God was faithful to all of my prayers.

The next week was filled with phone calls to notify friends and make funeral plans. I kept a safe distance from Mom, always making sure I put other people between us. Once the funeral was over and my siblings returned to their own homes, I went home to rest. I waited for my mother to call, hoping she would want to know how I was doing, but the phone never rang. For eleven months, the call never came. I felt impressed by the Lord not to pursue her but to leave her alone and let her make the next move. She never moved in my direction, but she did keep picking up the phone to talk to anyone else who would listen. She would vent her angry feelings against me. It was painful. I lost both my parents that year.

Daddy passed away in January, and several months later in April, we all attended the wedding of a nephew. It would be the first time our family had come together since Daddy's death. I love my family, and I did my part to not let the strain between Mom and me affect the celebration of the coming days. On the day of the wedding, Mom took her place as the proud grandmother on the second row while I sat about five rows back.

After the service and before we all left for the reception, I stood in the foyer with family. From the corner of my eye, I could see that Mom was seated a few feet away. Again I asked God if I should pursue her, if I should be the one to turn and melt the iceberg between us. God answered, "Do not move in her direction." So I continued enjoying the fellowship of my family and our friends.

When I walked into the reception hall, I noticed that tables were set aside for the family. Choosing to not get in the way, I went off to one side to mingle with old friends. Mom took her place as one of the grandmothers at the family table. My brother, Leroy, and his wife, Brandy, joined me, and we enjoyed the reception together. This brother had also been wounded by Mom during Dad's dying days, so he understood my choice to keep my distance from her, but Brandy had had enough. She told me that she was going over to Mom to see how much longer this would go on, and I told her to go for it.

She returned with the smile wiped right off her face. Her words were, "This is not going to be over for a long, long time. Your Mom is so angry." This news saddened me and felt like a punch to the stomach, but it didn't surprise me. Mom was still carrying a bitter grudge because I had stood up to her that day at Dad's bedside in the hospital. My childhood was being played out again like it was yesterday—I could feel her insensitive bullying. I succumbed to the disappointment and somehow made it through the reception.

God's Personal Message To Me

That evening I found myself wrestling with the hurt of my mother's comments. My heart was in pain; I was literally nauseated. I told the Lord I didn't know what to do, and I asked him to come and ease my pain. I felt him validate the wounding and tell me to go to bed and rest; he'd talk to me about it in the morning. The next day was Sunday.

I rested well that night, and the next morning I sat in church ready to enjoy the praise and worship. Little did I know that one of the songs was about to carry a personal message to me from God! The Lord answered me during a song titled "Every Knee Shall Bow." As I sang the words, "Every knee shall bow, and every tongue confess that Jesus Christ is Lord," God broke in with a vision. I saw two groups of people bowing before Jesus on judgment day.

In the first group were people who believed in God and served him faithfully. These people looked on Jesus and fell to their knees in awe of him. The second group was made up of people who were stubborn and didn't want to believe in Jesus. This group stood for a moment, and then they were made to submit when the Spirit's hand was placed on the back of their necks. His sovereign hand was pressing them to their knees. Every knee did bow, and every tongue did confess that Jesus was Lord. One group had grateful hearts while the second group had hearts filled with regrets. I knew my mother was in the second group.

My heart instantly became burdened for my mother, because I knew she was one who never wanted to believe in Jesus. Then the Lord spoke to my heart telling me to make a choice: I could either carry the offense of my mom's actions or carry the burden of her lost soul. The choice was mine to make. What was it going to be? I loved God with all my heart and wanted to serve him more than anything, and his heart breaks for those who turn their backs on him. I felt a strong burden for Mom's soul, and at that very moment, the sick feeling in my stomach left.

After I made the decision to carry the burden of my mother in my heart, I turned to my son, Timothy, who was seated next to me, and I told him what the Lord had just challenged me with. Tim knew about my heartache, and he'd been praying for me. I felt the Lord speak to my heart again. He told me he was pleased with my choice. He said if I had continued to walk in the offense—if I carried fear, resentment, and malice—then these emotions would keep me from sensing his presence. Then he asked, "What have I told you that you can do with all your burdens?" I answered him, "You said I can give all my burdens to you." God promises he will not just walk with us when we are burdened, but that he would also take our burdens upon himself. Isn't he amazing? I love him so. I was instantly released of the heaviness in my heart, and peace took its place.

This experience was in April, and Mom and I didn't talk until December. I was in a store the day before Christmas Eve, and as I passed by a display of beautiful Christmas arrangements, I heard the Lord tell me to send one of those arrangements to my mother. I bought one, and the next day Timothy stopped in to visit his Nana and give her the flowers. I was nervous about what her response would be. Would she even accept it? She had done some ugly things during the early part of those eleven months. She had never offered me any of the personal items that belonged to my dad; she gave them all to other family members. Then a few months after Dad died, she cut down the tree he and I had planted when my first child was born. Together Dad and I had loved watching that tree grow along with his grandchild. It was special to both of us. And a few weeks after Dad's death, she had one of my children return all the important personal papers I had been keeping in their home safe. She said she wasn't going to keep them any longer.

An hour or so later my phone rang and it was her. I chose not to answer the phone, and I let the answering machine pick up the call. She called to say thank you and asked me to call her back. It took a while before I could call, but I did finally, and we had a nice conversation. She never mentioned the confrontation at Daddy's bedside, and I felt safe inviting her to Christmas dinner with my children and friends. We never talked about that incident—at least she never talked to me about it—even though she talked to others. That was Mom; she was never going to change. But something changed inside me. I had gained new ground by standing up to her, and I was healed of the emotional injury that day in church. I was never going to let her bully me again. She tried, but I stood my ground for the next eight years.

Mom Is Gone

In fall of 2009, Mom's health really started to decline, and for several months it was touch and go, with trips to the emergency room and hospitalizations. I found her in a few distressing situations and was glad that I could be close by to help her. Twice she fell and was not able to get up until I found her. She found it comforting to not be alone, and she always commented on my efficiency. By June of 2010, she was much better, so I headed out of state to spend a little time with my children and their families. A few days into my vacation I received a call from my sister: "Mom is gone, Patti! Mom just passed away at home!" I couldn't believe my ears.

I had taken Mom in for a checkup just three weeks earlier, and her doctor was pleased to see how well she was doing. I felt it was safe to leave her for a little respite of my own. Now my children and I had to pack and caravan back to Colorado Springs. The trip, taking a day and a half, allowed us time to process our feelings and talk about our memories. I made numerous calls from the road to my siblings and to notify friends.

I needed and wanted to know how Mom died and what her last moments were like. I truly wasn't expecting her to slip away when I wasn't looking, so I began asking questions and putting the pieces together.

I first talked to my brother, Mike, and his wife the night Mom died. They were the first family members to arrive at her home after the neighbors found her. Mike had a routine of calling Mom every night around nine to check in with her and say good night. That night he decided to call a little early, around eight. When Mom didn't answer the phone, he called our friend Sherri, who lived next door to Mom, and asked her to go check on Mom. Mike just didn't feel right about the situation and headed over to Mom's house. When Sherri entered, she found Mom in front of the couch. Sherri pressed the medical alert button that hung around Mom's neck and waited for help to arrive. A few minutes later, the paramedics arrived, with Mike right behind them. There he saw Mom on the floor, on her back, in front of the couch. Once the paramedics confirmed she was gone, he began to call the family.

My sister-in-law spoke with such gentle words of comfort to me that night when she told me that Mom had looked so peaceful. You have to understand that Mom's last year was less than peaceful. She had a constant scowl on her face, and her comments were always negative. Mom would wake up angry, disappointed that she was still alive. Despite the encouraging words through calls and home visits from family and friends, she had chosen to sulk. To know Mom's final expression was that of peace meant the world to me. I knew that God had visited her those final moments. The coroner stated that there was no sign of struggle, and he ruled her death as a heart attack.

I arrived back in town two days later with my children and grandchildren. The first visit I made was to my mother's closest friend who lived down the street. Mrs. Spence was eager to share her experience with me about the night Mom passed away. My mother had become part of her daily routine as she stopped in to visit her around five each evening. This particular evening, Mrs. Spence arrived on Mom's front porch to find the front door closed and the mail still in the mail slot. Mom lived for the afternoon mail. Mrs. Spence rang the doorbell several times, and after a few moments decided that Mom wasn't home. Thinking that maybe family had taken Mom to dinner, she pushed the mail through the slot and walked back home. A few hours later she received the shocking phone call from my sister-in-law.

Again, I began to wonder about Mom's final moments. It

made me sad to know that Mom's body was undiscovered for several hours. I had questions: Did she lie there afraid, crying out for someone to help? Did she ask God into her life? Where was her soul? It made my heart feel heavy, but I had to switch gears and care for family because they were in grief, and we had funeral arrangements to make. So I tucked Mrs. Spence's story into my heart alone with the information my sister-in-law had given me.

My next visit was with Sherri, our friend who lived next door to Mom. Sherri told me that she had placed her hand on Mom's throat, and she was still warm to the touch. After Sherri pressed the medical alert button, she began CPR. This troubled me. If Mom didn't come to the door at five, but her body was still warm a little after eight, shouldn't she have been cold to the touch?

This wasn't a heart attack; she'd had a stroke. It made me sad to think that Mom had lain there in that condition for those long hours. Once again, I kept my thoughts to myself and comforted my friend who was in tears as she told me her experience.

We buried Mom on a Tuesday and then began to send family members on their way home over the next few days. I wanted to be in church that following Sunday, so off I went. Remember, I still had some unanswered questions in my heart about Mom's final hours. During the praise and worship, the Lord talked to me. He showed me through a vision just how he'd held my mother during the stroke and in those final hours. He talked to her about her life. They reasoned together, and she submitted to him. She accepted him as her personal Savior.

Now here's the most precious part. I didn't tell you how Sherri found Mom. Mom was not lying on the floor when Sherri came into the house—that's what my brother and his wife saw. *Lori Wells was on bended knees in front of her couch!*

Every knee shall bow and every tongue confess that Jesus Christ is Lord (paraphrase from Philippians 2:10–11).

Chapter 2

My Young Life

I Was Given My Name

I arrived the first week of a very hot August. The name on the birth certificate was *Patricia Ann*. I had a full head of dark hair and long eyelashes. In fact, the first comment the doctor made to my mother was, "Look at those long eyelashes!" Twenty-four years later, I would hear my doctor make the same comment to me when my daughter was born. She too had a full head of dark hair and long eyelashes. Isn't it interesting how things can repeat themselves from one generation to the next?

Five dollars and thirty-six cents was the first investment my father made in my life, according to the invoice placed in his hand at the time of my release from the hospital nursery. I was born into a military family in Fort Benning, Georgia. My father served in the Army for twenty-eight years, while my mother remained home as a housewife. They met in 1951 while dad was stationed in Stuttgart, Germany.

My mom was born in Germany. She could remember standing in her family's living room at nine years old, hearing the news that her beloved Germany was now at war. She was eleven when the bombs literally began to fall on her head. My dad was an enlisted mechanic from Kentucky, stationed in her area after the war. We always laughed about the fact that Mom married a "ridge runner" from Kentucky; I would tell everyone that makes me a "German hillbilly."

Throughout my fifty-six years on planet earth, I've experienced some unrelenting hardships, and I credit my natural strength to my parents' example. Both my parents saw the depths of evil that can lie in the human heart, so they learned to turn off their emotions to survive. I heard my mother say on many occasions that she didn't know which was worse: living through the bombings for four years or the hunger and rebuilding that followed for the next three years. Germany was a mess after the war with high unemployment, food shortages, and despair underlying everything.

My father was on the other side of the war she experienced. Mom was a civilian, and Dad was an enlisted mechanic turned medic. He did his tour of duty during World War II in India, Africa, and Germany as a mechanic, and then became a medic before his tour in Korea and Vietnam. He returned from Vietnam a quiet man. I know only a few of his stories. They were examples of strength and courage from human effort.

My parents worked hard to keep us connected to both sides of their families. When I was three, we were transferred to Fort Carson, Colorado, where my family remained for fifty-three years. I don't remember too much of my childhood. What I do know I've learned from pictures I've seen and stories people have shared. To others it might have seemed like a happy childhood, but I don't remember it that way. Many sad things happened to me, things no child should have to experience or endure.

My mother was full of rage because of the hardships of her childhood in war-torn Germany. She never sought professional help to deal with her memories or bad dreams. Her anger could be ignited at any moment, for any reason. There was no pattern to her behavior, so I lived ready for an explosion from sunrise to sunset. As I grew older and physically bigger, the physical abuse became less, but Mom rechanneled her rage into sarcasm. Cruel, cold sarcasm flowed from her mouth every day of my life.

The Plate

I vividly remember an incident that happened when I was in kindergarten. It was the first negative impact from my mother that I can remember, and for years it was the cause of depression in my spirit. I was the third child and oldest girl. I remember a silver plate with scalloped edges that always sat on the coffee table. The plate held plastic fruit or flowers, depending on the season. Mom liked the plate placed in the center of the table. Small ashtrays sat on either side, and pretty candles finished the five-piece display. For whatever reason, I would look at the plate and feel that it needed to be slightly turned from its original position. I must have moved it one too many times because this time I really made Mom explode.

In one swift move she threw that plate at me with all her might. I remember seeing it fly across the room toward me;

instinctively I tried to duck, but the plate caught me right between the eyes, cutting deep into the ridge of my nose. I must have been knocked out because I don't remember being taken to the hospital.

My next memory was that of lying face up on a gurney in the emergency room. A sterile cloth was draped over my face with a small opening just around my nose. I could peek out from the hole, and as I did, I saw the doctor's hand coming toward my face to place a stitch, and then his hand would pull away to tighten the stitch. I remember crying as I lay very still and the doctor praising me for being a brave little girl.

I could sense that Dad was standing on my left side and that Mom wasn't in the room. I don't remember too much more—the ride home or my mother comforting me. I've always wondered what Dad had to say to her about hurting me so. What story did he tell the staff at the emergency room about how I had received my injury?

Years later, Mom would bring the incident up. She talked about how I could really irritate her, and then she'd remind me of the plate. Never once did she apologize. In fact, she made it clear that it was my fault I got hurt so badly. She was only going to hit me in the stomach with the plate, but I was the one who ducked. Her warped logic never accounted for the wound I received. It wouldn't have mattered where her metal Frisbee landed; mothers are supposed to protect their children.

On too many occasions she would come bursting into my bedroom because she thought I was making too much noise or I didn't answer her fast enough when she called me. With hatred in her face and through clinched teeth, she would beat me with whatever object she'd picked up on her way into my room. The message I heard loud and clear was: I have to be a good girl or she's going to kill me. For the rest of her life I worked hard to not make her mad at me.

My New Church Family

When I was in kindergarten, family friends asked if they could take my brothers, sister, and me to church. That's when my life became tolerable. The church, filled with complete strangers, became my sanctuary from my home life. Those saints were kind to me, gentle and pleasant to be around. Sunday school teachers showed me love and a different kind of life. These ladies called me by my name and used terms of endearment like "angel eyes" or "my Patti girl." I received hugs, lots and lots of hugs. Little by little, year after year, the fragmented pieces of my life were put back into proper order. My mother was never easy to live with, but I discovered a God who was so easy to live with, and I asked him into my heart. Once he was in my heart, I noticed he would go home with me.

God used that small Nazarene church in our neighborhood to protect and heal me. They didn't know how bad things were for me at home. *I* didn't know how bad things were for me at home, because I thought it was normal. I made sure I was in church every time the doors were open. You'd find me there every Sunday morning and evening, every Wednesday night, every revival, and all the Vacation Bible Schools. I wasn't there because I was a great student of the Bible. I was there because church was a safer place to be than home. Little did those precious people know that their unconditional love covered me with a protective shield, a shield that I carried with me as I walked back into my house. Those church ladies lavished so much love on me that it spilled over when I was with my family. Who knows? Maybe because people were watching me closely, my mom backed off physically abusing me, afraid it would leave bruises on me.

God Was with Me

Years later as an adult and while attending some counseling classes, I had a powerful breakthrough about the plate assault. For the first time in my life, I stirred up the courage to ask God, "Where were you?" Where was he when the abuse was happening in my home? I was always afraid to ask God such a direct question, but as I grew in knowledge of his kindness, I learned that I could come to him with anything. He already saw the question hiding in a corner of my mind, so he encouraged me to say it out loud. And when I did, he didn't get mad. He said, "I'm glad you asked. Now let me show you right where I was." With those words came instant revelation. Once again, I was back in the emergency room on the gurney with the doctor stitching my nose, and I was peeking out of the corner of the cloth. All my life I'd had a limited view that wouldn't let me see past my own nose. Satan's minions had attempted to make sure that was all I would ever see and all I would ever understand.

In the vision, I went from lying on the table to sitting in an observation room elevated above the emergency room. I could see the gurney, the doctor standing on the right side, and my father standing on the left side. Then for the first time I saw right where God was! He was standing at the head of the gurney, his left hand was on my little shoulder, and he was stroking my forehead with his right hand. My heavenly Father was comforting his little girl. He was saddened by the incident and was comforting me. Then I had another vision. I heard the doctor say, "She's one lucky girl; just a little more to the right or the left and she could have damaged an eye!" God's right hand blocked for me that day. He drew a line in the sand and spoke to the spirit of anger in my mother's heart, "That's far enough, no more!" God turned that plate into a platter that symbolizes his love, protection, and grace. I have eaten from his silver platter from that day on.

This book is not intended to bring disrespect to any of the people in my life. I love my family, and I know I was placed right in the middle of them for reasons you'll discover later. But I want to lay some groundwork, so you'll know where I'm coming from in the following chapters.

There's a real enemy of our soul, and he has been after us from the beginning. But we have a *Hero* more powerful than this enemy! A God who knows me by name. In fact, he gave me my name. Patricia means "Woman of noble character." I was thrilled the day I discovered what my name meant. For sixteen years I thought it meant "jackass." That is the endearing term Mom used to describe me.

My mother and me when I was a baby.

Me at three years old.

Me in kindergarten.

Chapter 3

Growing Up

Someone Please Say You Love Me

I don't remember hearing Mom say "I love you" until I was almost sixteen years old. I had reconstructive foot surgery the summer I started high school, and when my mother was allowed to see me in the recovery room, she leaned over my bed and said, "I love you." The sad part was that I didn't respond. I had endured years of her mean words and spirit, and I wanted to hurt her, so I chose to stay silent. I didn't say "I love you" back to her. In my heart I wanted to shun her, and it felt good to have some power over her.

For whatever reason, I had become a target for sexual predators. The first time I heard the words "I love you," I was in the fourth grade, and I was being molested. He was in high school. The first encounter wasn't forced; I liked the attention. It was twisted, but I was hungry for what I thought was love.

The second predator inflicted the most horrific pain on me. I was still in the fourth grade, and he was in high school. I was so hungry for attention that he was able to draw me in several times. It was playful at first, but then the activity turned painful, so I tried to stay away from him. Because he lived next door to us, it was difficult to avoid him.

I encountered several more assaults, but in seventh grade one assault sent the most damaging message to my young soul. The man was my dad's army buddy, and he was old enough to be my father. Our two families spent a lot of time together when the fathers weren't working, and while my father never harmed me in this capacity, his friend had been inappropriate with me numerous times.

I tried to dodge this man for two and a half years, but then he received orders to deploy to Vietnam. Just before he was to leave, he had his wife call my mother to ask if I could come over to help out with their younger boys while they packed his things.

Mom dropped me off to spend the morning in their home. He cornered me in the dining room and pinned me against the table. My back was against it, and I was facing the entrance to the hallway. He was on me—his adult mouth on my little child's mouth. I was frozen in place, and with eyes wide open, I watched his wife walk in on us and then quickly back out down the hallway. His back was to her, so he never knew she had come in and slipped out. But I knew then that no one was going to protect me or stand up for me. My little girl's heart received and believed the message that no one cared about me. I felt invisible. It was a crippling message I carried deep inside me for a long, long time.

I never told my parents about my predators because I knew they would have somehow made it be my fault. They would have asked me what I did to encourage that behavior. So I remained silent for years. My little sister didn't know anything until we became young mothers. When I brought up the sexual abuse to my parents a few years later, Mom became angry. She made sure I knew how much I had hurt Dad and her. She told one of my brothers that she didn't believe it was true. But she never asked how I felt.

The love I experienced in life was based on my performance. As long as I served or pleased people, I believed I would be loved. That fact even played out in my twenty-five-year marriage to my high school sweetheart. I wasn't aware of his sexual addiction, but in order to hear the words "I love you" from him, I had to be performing sexually. I didn't know enough then to know that it was wrong—it was normal for me. It's a sad way to live; but it's how I survived. My survival skills became my dysfunction later. The following chapters will tell how I broke away from the mindset that I had to perform to be loved or accepted.

I'll always be grateful for the unconditional love I felt from the church, which was the prelude to knowing God's unconditional love for me. At church I was taught a precious song that says, "Jesus loves me this I know, for the Bible tells me so. *Little ones to him belong.* They are weak, but he is strong." I used to sing this song with great purpose to myself as a child. Then, I sang it to my children, and now I sing it to my grandchildren.

I was twenty-four years old when I finally experienced deep, unconditional love from another human. It came from an interesting little person, a person who couldn't speak a single word to me at first—a person who couldn't do anything for me, but only look with adoration into my eyes and into my heart. My children have been the saving point for me. Their first words were Momma, their first gifts were kisses and hugs and silly dandelions from the yard. I did not have to perform for them to have their love.

My three babies helped me to release a portion of the hurtful things from my past so that I could move forward. I chose *on purpose* to love the people in my life and never make them guess about how I felt about them.

Where Was Your Dad?

I know that's a question you've been asking yourself as you read the first part of my story. You can imagine a little girl named Patti, and you've drawn a picture of her mother in your mind, but it's unclear where her dad was during all of the chaos. It's an easy answer. My father had turned off his emotions and faded into the background of my life. Not just my life, but also his own life.

His wife, my mother, was not easy on him. Because of her unresolved resentment toward him, she rarely appreciated his commitment to her. In fact, there were times when she abused that commitment and emotionally blackmailed him with it, threatening to divorce him because she knew of his strong stand against it.

In the 1940s, society frowned on the scandal of divorce. Disapproval of divorce was especially strong in the small townships of Kentucky. My father's parents divorced when he was a young man, and it tore a big hole in his heart. They separated because his mother left him, his father, and two brothers for another man. My father made a silent vow as a young man that he would never put his children through the pain and disgrace of divorce. He would never leave his children, under any circumstance. On the other hand, I was praying for a divorce because I would gladly have gone to live with my dad.

Remember how my parents met? She was a young German girl living in Stuttgart, Germany, and Dad was a young and wild soldier stationed at the army base just on the outskirts of the city. Their relationship quickly became physical, and Mom became pregnant. It was something my dad didn't expect, and he had a decision to make. He had met too many young German women who had given themselves to military men because they were promised love, only to be abandoned by them once there was a pregnancy. He saw how the women and children had to face society with the shame of an out-of-wedlock pregnancy, abandonment, and the pain of a broken heart. My father, John Wells, made an unshakable vow to himself. He would never leave his child. He married my mother, and together they had five children over the next seven years.

Because of the unhealthy patterns in his own family, my father lived for other people and neglected to nurture himself or find what made him happy and satisfied. He was either unaware or afraid of his own feelings. He feared rejection and didn't like conflict or anger, so he would avoid saying or doing certain things. I loved him very much because he was the kinder of my two parents, and as a young person I was impressed by his work ethic—how hard he worked and the long hours he spent away from home providing for us. I later came to realize he used work to avoid my mother and her unsatisfied demands. I was disappointed in him because he never stood up to Mom. I used to daydream that John Wayne was my father, because he would have set my mother straight! John Wayne was a man's man, so different from my passive dad who seemed almost nonexistent to me.

Dad's behavior was damaging for me. He modeled weakness and expected me to submit to Mom as he did. While I was in counseling around the age of thirty-four, I realized that my decorated war-veteran father was a coward. I didn't want to think of him that way, and it hurt me to have to say that about him. Because his emotional needs were never met, Dad turned his emotions off and went into a survival mode. He was handling his life—just getting by without feelings, and that was enough. I too developed this survival mode and turned my emotions off as well.

The Dad I Never Knew

Even though my dad didn't stand up to Mom, I found out later there were times when he had stood up to life heroically. Just shortly after he died at age eighty, we received an amazing letter from a retired military man. This veteran had served with my father in Vietnam. He had been only nineteen years old at the time. Darrell wanted to share an experience he'd had with Dad in February 1970. He and my father were attached to a medical unit. The weather was horrible as typhoon weather grounded all helicopters, so they were called to transport wounded men to the hospital in Chu Lia—men with open chest wounds, gunshot wounds, and temperatures of 105 degrees. The roads were treacherous, and snipers were reported along the road leading into the area where the injured men were located.

Dad assigned Darrell to be the driver, while he posted himself to ride shotgun. Darrell said he had never been more scared in his life, but my father kept him calm with encouraging words. With sixty-mile-per-hour winds, they drove the big truck through fender-deep waters, while dad, the door gunner, protected his passengers from rooftop gunfire. It took two hours to reach the injured troops, but their mission was successful. Darrell received an accommodation medal for his role that night. In fact, he stated that he had received three medals during his tour, all for hostile fire, and all three while joined by my dad.

My father was a very private man. We were stunned to find all his medals discretely placed in a simple shoebox on the top of his closet. A box filled with bronze stars and many other accommodations. I wish I knew more of his stories. Mom never bragged about him or his accomplishments; she just highlighted his weaknesses and her unrealistic expectations.

My dad was an emotionally injured man with needs buried

deep inside himself. My needs were never met at home either. How could they be when the two people who were raising me were so wounded themselves? That's when my Hero came to my rescue. No, I'm not talking about John Wayne. God came. He became my precious Father through the men of my childhood church. Those men didn't know a little girl was watching them closely. I watched how they led their families. Respect looks good on a man, and their wives respected them. I watched these Christian men pray for their children and serve the community. I even saw them cry when they were blessed or burdened. I absolutely loved how they noticed me and included me in their family activities. This was the kind of man I wanted to marry. I wanted to have a family with this kind of man. I'll always be grateful to God for showing up in the examples of these good men.

My childhood.

Mom in front of 509 Stevens Avenue.

My family.

My siblings and me.

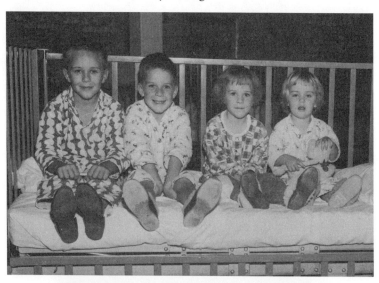

Chapter 4

School Days

The Dummy Class

School was a place of academic torment for me. From my first day of kindergarten I found it difficult to stay focused. I tried, but I couldn't seem to concentrate. I was below the national average. Red is supposed to be an exciting color used for roses, Valentines, and Christmas, but I hated seeing those red correction marks on my papers. I was two grade levels behind in elementary school and kept falling behind as the years passed. By the time I graduated from high school, I could read only at the seventh-grade level.

I really wanted to be a smart person. Smart kids were all

around me, and I wanted to be one of them. I saw how the teacher praised them in front of the class, and I saw all their rewards. But I never took any home. Too many times I sat in school assemblies hoping they might call my name also. Whenever a teacher told us we were having a spelling bee, my stomach dropped, because I knew I'd be one of the first to sit down.

There was no way out of my humiliation except through humor. I became the class clown, and instead of people laughing at me, I made them laugh with me. It was the only control I had, and I became quite witty.

When I was in fourth grade, my teacher arranged for me to take a supplementary reading class taught by Mrs. Hall and held outside the school building in a trailer. Mrs. Hall was crippled in her hips and walked with a profound limp. The students described her as the crippled lady who ran the "dummy trailer." Now I found myself going to the dummy trailer to be taught by the crippled lady. My self-esteem, what was left of it, was demolished.

Mrs. Hall was a sweet lady who had a kind voice. She always had encouraging things to say to the students in her classroom. I loved her attention and wanted to please her. She assigned each of us a paper cutout of an astronaut. She wrote each of our names on a cutout and posted them on the wall near the ceiling. I loved looking at the cluster of astronauts starting out in the far corner of the room. Mrs. Hall's goal was for our astronauts to travel through the universe of education, from one corner of the room all the way around to the finish line. Soon I realized my astronaut was not doing well; I had fallen behind all the others. When I didn't think I could feel any worse about myself, I did. I was in the dummy trailer, trailing way behind the other dummies. I felt so brainless. I'm not sure how I coped all those years. I guess that's why I became such a helpful student. I received my rewards through the compliments teachers gave me for being such a sweet little helper.

Thoughts of Suicide

By the time I was thirteen years old, the insanity of my life took its toll. The sexual, physical, and verbal abuse had drained all the life out of me, and school made me feel like an invisible dummy, not worth anyone's time. It seemed like people walked right through me to get to the events of their day. I had no one fighting for me, but instead, I felt like I was fighting them all off. I wanted to escape the nothingness of my life, and

I began to think of suicide as a way out of the pain. My coping mechanism at that point was to live in a fantasy world. In my daydreams, I was pretty and smart, my father noticed me and protected me, and my mother was kind and wanted me. But after so many years, the fantasies grew empty. I felt unloved and unprotected by the adults around me, and I despaired of life.

God seemed distant to me. My friends faithfully brought me to church; I sat with my girlfriends' families as an adopted child. The pastor sat up on the platform, and God sat somewhere high above us all. He was untouchable. I could sense a peaceful presence, and that's what drew me into church again and again. Church was a safe place for me.

I thought of God the same way I thought of my school principal. I knew of the principal, but didn't really know him, never interacted with him even though he knew me. I was always with my friends and teachers, but I knew he had the authority over us and that the welfare of the kids was his priority.

My Plan—God's Plan

I had it all planned out. After the family went to bed that night, I would go into the bathroom where Mom kept her medications. I was going to take as many as I could find and then go lie down in my bed to die. I was convinced that no one cared for me and no one would even notice. I was so unhappy on planet earth, I might as well just leave. Everything about my life was sad and horribly disappointing. I thought death couldn't be as painful as living.

I reached bottom right there in my childhood bedroom. It was after dinner, and I was alone in my room. With the door closed, I sat on the lower bunk. For the first time in my life, I felt an urgency to pick up the Bible my parents had given me. I had taken it to church, and the adults would read to me, but I'd never been drawn to the Scriptures myself. Neither Mom nor Dad ever prayed—at least that I knew of—and I never saw them read the Bible. I thought you read the Bible like you would a schoolbook you use to do your homework. I had never known its power. After that night it wasn't about me reading it anymore. It was about that book *reading me*! It read right into my heart.

I opened my Bible to Psalm 139 and read the chapter. Oh, the impact those Scriptures had on me! I highlighted with a red marker every word that jumped out at me. Verses 1–5 thrilled my heart as I read:

O LORD, you have searched me and you know me.
You know when I sit and when I rise;
You perceive my thoughts from afar.
You discern my going out and my lying down;
You are familiar with all my ways.
Before a word is on my tongue you know it completely,
O LORD.
You hem me in—behind and before;
You have laid your hand upon me.

Verses 13–16 also spoke to me:
For you created my inmost being;
You knit me together in my mother's womb.
I praise you because I am fearfully and wonderfully made;
Your works are wonderful, I know that full well.
My frame [Patricia Ann's body] was not hidden from you
when I was made in the secret place.
When I was woven together in the depths of the earth,
your eyes saw my unformed body.
All the days ordained for me were written in your book
before one of them came to be.

I read the chapter again, and this time I began to cry. My tears fell on the page, causing the red marker to run. By the time I was done with this revelation moment, my Bible looked like a bloody battle had taken place. And you know what? A battle in the heavens had taken place for my soul and my very being! God was no longer out there in the great somewhere. He was sitting next to me on my bunk bed. His arm was around me, and he was reading to me from his living Word. Do you know the impact those Scriptures had on this "invisible dummy?" To have *the God of the universe* take time to come to where I was sitting on my bunk bed that night?

That night, I believed that God existed, that I mattered to him, and that he had the power to help me get through the rest of my life. The truth that he knew me shook me to the core and awakened in me a new passion for life. God's Holy Spirit was sealed into my spirit that night; God does not bring us into this life without a purpose. I saw for the first time that he knit me together with all my strengths and weaknesses.

God has personally seen me through every situation life has thrown at me, and thoughts of suicide have never returned. The Bible says "'For I know the plans I have for you' declares the Lord, 'plans to prosper you and not harm you, plans to give you hope and a future'" (Jeremiah 29:11), and I made plans that night to stay around and see all that God had planned for me!

Working by Age Fourteen

The summer is supposed to be a time off from school to enjoy a vacation break, but my Mom volunteered me to become a caregiver for an elderly woman dying of cancer. Her husband was a fire chief who needed to work due to medical bills. The year was 1970, and we, as a society, didn't talk about cancer. Her husband chose not to tell her she was dying, and I was instructed not to say a word. It was hard to hear her making plans for her life once her illness was over. I worked from eight in the morning until four in the afternoon five days a week, and I earned an impressive fifty cents an hour. I thought I was going to be a companion, sitting close by in case she needed anything. Instead, I worked like a dog.

My house cleaning chores went way beyond dusting and doing dishes. I prepared her breakfast and lunch and their dinner, scrubbed floors, washed windows, cleaned out closets, did laundry, ironed clothes, and learned how to starch his uniforms. Just the way every fourteen-year-old girl wants to spend her summer—away from friends, in a dark and dismal house with a dying woman. My friends would ride by on their bikes yelling, "Hello, Patti!" They were enjoying their summer break.

I felt like my mother's prize workhorse. She loved bragging to her girlfriends about her hard-working daughter. I didn't realize until years later that I was her personal Cinderella, because she had me working just as hard at home.

She also found me a second job that summer. I bussed tables at a local restaurant three evenings a week. It turned out to be a lot of fun because I had a great time with my peers. It felt satisfying to learn new skills and interact with the public. All through the year Mom also found babysitting jobs for me on the weekends. I began to appreciate the time out of my home and the money I could earn. My life was full with school, church, and work. I used these activities to avoid being home.

Once I got to high school, I applied for a program to earn credit hours by working off campus. My last two years of high school I took morning classes, and then after lunch with my peers, I'd work in a fabric store. I enjoyed my job there. I had acquired a talent for sewing while in junior high home economic classes, and I absolutely loved creating a complete garment from a piece of fabric. But I had to work twice as hard as my coworkers in order to read the information about different products, concepts, and manufacturing.

I discovered my gift of communication when I had to bluff my way through a lot of situations. I could coach a customer through her project, because God gave me wisdom and insight to share my talent with others and motivate them to do their best. I made sewing doable for them, and it was a great feeling. I had begun to learn the way of wisdom and it countered my lack of academic skills.

Because of my good work ethic, jobs came easy to me. I had found my niche in life; I loved retail, and I liked people. I could have chosen to become a mean-spirited person and driven people away from me. But through different jobs and great managers, I learned about the rewards of treating people kindly. My employers complimented my talents and challenged me to do new things. It was a great feeling.

I instilled the principle of strong work ethic in my children. I also let my children choose the type of work they wanted to do, and I encouraged them to try even when they felt uneasy about their abilities. The Davis family can always find resourceful ways to make a living. We serve a God who says he will bless whatever we lay our hands on as long as we continue to honor him first.

When God measured me, he didn't put a tape measure around my head, he put it around my heart. I had lots of heart.

My room.

Chapter 5

The Church Ladies

Safe and Trustworthy

When I think about the women who taught me in Sunday school and the mothers of my girlfriends, I think about how safe they were. They nurtured me; they were trustworthy, and I felt lovable around them. They were my spiritual mothers, and I wanted to walk in their footsteps. My parents raised me in hostility, but these ladies taught me by example that I could raise my own children in a peaceful environment. They were a blessing in my life that would be lived out in the generations that came from me.

If there were wrongs done to you in your life, I want to encourage you that God can help you to right the wrongs. Don't pass them on to your children, the next generation, like my grandmother and mother chose to do. My grandmother, like my mother, was unaffectionate and showed favoritism of one child over another. Again, I don't want to harm my mother; I'm testifying about my very big God.

I felt safe with these good women because they were predictable and danger-free. I learned through counseling that without a safe person, a child remains in a state of panic or anxiety and is unable to love and learn. These ladies never raised a hand to strike me. Instead, they would hold my face in their hands and fuss over me. God used those ladies to transform the dangerous world into a place of safety. I was protected by their prayers, and I was determined to be a safe mother when I grew up.

I heard a pastor once say that a mother's nurture is fuel for the soul. Good mothers pour care into the souls of their children like a gardener pours care into the soil of his plants. Our souls flourish when we are cared for. We grow, develop, and change according to the way we were designed. What happens to a plant that goes without nurture? It withers. A plant needs sun, water, and fertilizer. But too much fertilizer can kill a plant. That's where my Mom went into overkill—too much *fertilizer* came from her mouth. Not only was I an irritation and a "jackass" to her, she let me know that I wouldn't be able to get along with even Jesus Christ himself! I told people that my mother spoke three languages fluently: German, English, and sarcasm.

The church ladies spoke words of life over me. I loved how they would pray out loud for me, so I could hear them talking to God about me. It definitely nurtured my dry soul. As a young mother, I chose to speak life-giving words to my children. I guarded my children from my family's sarcasm, and my heart absolutely melted hearing my children's schoolteachers say, "Your child has great self-esteem."

The word *trust* is "the ability to invest oneself in a relationship." We are not born trusting; trust is learned. When we trust we are able to reach out, to depend, to need, and to see others as the source of good things. The enemy of my soul made sure my childhood experiences shut me down and closed my heart to ever trusting people.

I couldn't trust my mother with my heart or my good intentions, but the women of the church were trustworthy, and they let me depend on them when I reached out. I let myself need them without fear. As a mother, I ache for my children to know that they could depend on me when they reach out. I want them to find the Spirit of God when they come to me, and to find God trustworthy for themselves, as he has proved himself to me through his Word and countless experiences.

We all need to belong to someone and to something bigger than ourselves. *Belonging* is another need that was met by the church, and through their love and care I felt wanted. This made me feel worthwhile. Because I experienced being consistently wanted, I was able to move easily into other relationships, never wondering if I belonged or not. God still lets me know every day that I belong to him.

The ladies also taught me another truth: We have a basic need to love people, and that requires someone to love. I wasn't always to be on the receiving end of God's love, but I was called to pass it on. I needed to love others.

If a mother is safe, we respond with love for her. If she's not, we are either overwhelmed by isolation or we are filled with hatred—or both. I could have easily hated because of what I experienced with my mother. But the church ladies showed me a better way. Love filled me up and colored my outlook on others and the world, so that I viewed life with hope and optimism. These attitudes don't come from taking a vitamin supplement. They come from being loved and loving others. These women of my childhood provided me with an outlet to love. As a young mother, I always tried to tell my children that they were my pride and joy, and I've always thanked God out loud for them.

The Christian ladies came to my wedding and a few years later showered me with gifts as I started to have children. Most of those women have passed away now, but their influence continues to live on in my life and the lives of my family.

Mrs. Bridgewater

I've got to tell you about Mrs. Dorothy Bridgewater. In the Church of the Nazarene, she was highly respected. She and her husband were evangelists, and we were blessed to have them in our church. Mrs. Bridgewater was the first person to ever call me "angel eyes." She always sat on the left side of the sanctuary close to the front. I would watch her and her husband love God during praise and worship. This man and woman of God knew to whom they were praying.

At first and totally out of ignorance, I would poke fun at them in my mind. But as I began to mature in the Spirit, I came to realize that they were two of God's elite. His anointing was on them. She looked like an angel to me, and her love and respect for her husband impressed me so much.

One Sunday evening, the pastor led the congregation in a time of ministry and prayer. I was a sassy little teenage girl who hid in the cluster of our youth group. I was seated at the back of the church with other teens when Mrs. Bridgewater went on the move. It was common for her to quietly walk around the outer edges of the sanctuary and pray. This night she didn't walk in her normal route but headed to our group. She stopped at the end of my row, asking my girlfriends to step aside as she came straight to me. She held my face in her hands and asked me, "Is everything right with you and God?" I melted in her hands. Her tender concern brought a gentle confession from me that I could be doing better. She smiled and we prayed, and I fell in love with God all over again that night. He sent a personal message to me through that respected and anointed lady.

I look back at that night, and I believe that God let some

of her anointing flow onto me. Today I'm a teacher of the Bible, and I learned a lot from her and her bold teaching of the Word. On occasion my adult peers have even compared me to Mrs. Bridgewater.

Chapter 6

I Married My High School Sweetheart

George

George and I met at the school bus stop when we were just fourteen years old. He thought I was conceited, and I thought he was a big bully. At age fifteen he walked into my youth group at church, and I remember not being too happy about that. It was bad enough having this bully at my bus stop, but now he had come into my safe place—my church. As time moved on, we shared many church activities and slowly got to know each other. By our sophomore year in high school we were going steady, and I fell in love with him. We made a sharp-looking couple. On New Year's Eve of our senior year, George asked me to marry him, and we married twenty months later.

He was a welcome relief from my home life. We shared all the same friends in school and church, spent a lot of time together, and blended well with each other's families. His father had the same anger issues that my mother had, so we instantly bonded as survivors of "rageoholics." We were two broken people clinging to each other. We shared the same values toward life, work, family, and church. It all seemed so right to me!

George joined the military a year after graduating from high school, and his first tour was in Korea. With my parents' blessing, we put our wedding plans in high gear and wed just eight days before he was deployed. I planned to live at home with my parents for the year and save money for a nice nest egg when he returned. Three months into his tour, he sent for me, and we lived off base for six months. It was an amazing adventure. I had never been away from home, and I found myself living in a foreign country.

In the four years George and I dated, I had never seen him take a drink. But now that we were away from family and home, friends and church, I saw a side of him I didn't know existed.

The night of our six-month anniversary while we were out with friends, he almost drank himself under the table. On the way home he came close to starting a fight, and the evening ended with him openly urinating in front of everyone. They laughed, but I cried deep down inside because this wasn't my world. He bullied me into accepting his behavior and told me to lighten up. We had never had a reason to be disappointed in one another up to that point, but I lost respect for him that night.

I found out I was pregnant shortly after our fourth anniversary. We were thrilled. I loved children and was so excited about having my own baby. We went on to have three babies in the next four years. George was a good daddy. Our children brought us a great deal of joy and kept George and me connected.

The Affairs

As the years went by, our relationship began fading, but I just accepted it as a part of life. Our relationship was at least better than our parents' relationships. Church was a big part of our lives, and it preserved my sanity once again. Our youngest son was four years old when I felt George's heart turn cold toward me. For eleven months he didn't say the words "I love you."

He had become so distant. At first I thought I was the problem and tried hard to get him to warm up to me again. But it didn't work, and I found out why. He was having an affair with another man's wife. I died inside. Because of my unhealthy boundaries and my extreme fear of rejection, I worked hard to get George to change his attitudes and behavior. The experience of George's affair left a giant hole in my heart that never healed.

The only thing that could override the pain was my commitment to my children. They were my function in the dysfunctional marriage, and they filled my heart up with unconditional love as I lived in a loveless marriage. I raised our children with a big hole in my heart. Even when I found out about all the women George had been with, I didn't have the strength or confidence to leave him. I was under a false belief that told me the kids needed both their parents and I couldn't make it on my own. I felt trapped. After all, didn't he say he was sorry, and aren't Christian wives supposed to forgive?

George ended the affair and made a new commitment to me, but he just traded one addiction for another—he became a closet alcoholic. By the time our youngest was thirteen, the drinking had become too much. Our children were at the age of reasoning, and now they had tough questions about why I was allowing his behavior. So, I told George he had to leave. The boys were saddened when George moved out, but Chrystal was relieved, because her dad had publicly embarrassed her a few times. I had to preserve our sanity, and expelling George from the home was the avenue. It's not what I wanted, but it was a decision I needed to make.

There are times when chaos reigns in our lives because others are not willing or able to fulfill their God-given roles. When this happens, we often suffer from a lack of leadership and protection. I've always looked at men's hands. Their hands are important. They are tender when they touch our soft skin, strong when we need to be protected or guided, and skilled so they can provide for us. At least that's what I thought when I placed the wedding band on George's left hand. I chose him to care for me—until "death do us part." I wanted to be protected and cared for, but that is not what happened.

Dealing with Regrets

My heart was full of regrets about being his wife. When there are regrets, there is grief for loss and for the things left unsaid and undone. I had given myself to only one man, and I lost all those years to that one man; now I found myself alone. I didn't feel its full impact until my children married their spouses, and I saw the love they have for each other. I've never felt the love of a husband. I've watched other couples, and I'm glad for them, but I can't comprehend what they must feel. I witness it in my children's marriages, I see it portrayed in movies, and I envision it in stories, but I've not known it for myself. To this day, I don't listen to love songs because it hurts. I cry when I'm alone watching a romantic movie. I see the man gaze into his lady's eyes, but I've never had that. George always made me feel invisible.

It was a few years into my singleness that God broke through my regrets with his words. God responded to his people in Jerusalem as they cried out in regret that the Lord has deserted and forgotten them. In Isaiah 49: 15–16, God answered them:

> Can a mother forget the baby at her breast
> and have no compassion on the child she has borne?
> Though she may forget,
> I will not forget you!
> See, I have engraved you on the palms of my hands.

He showed me that his love is greater than the natural affection of a loving mother or husband. God has watched over me all these years with great tenderness and love, and he has been, and continues to be, my faithful husband. Through him I also have the love and respect of my friends' husbands and the elders in my church. I may not have one man caring for me, but God showed me I was a woman who has a garrison of men watching over me. All I have to do is cry out in need, and they will come to my aid. I am blessed among women!

George and me during our sophomore year in High School.

George and my engagement picture our Senior year.

Chapter 7

Cancer

Cancer Doesn't Scare Me Anymore!

My emotional wellbeing was shattered when I lost my belief that life was fair and I had control over it. The helplessness I felt pulled me toward a feeling of hopelessness, never stronger than the day after my biopsy. I was given the grim news when I woke up in recovery. It was cancer, and it had gone into the lymph nodes. My surgeon stood at my bed to deliver the news personally. He encouraged me to rest; we would talk later.

The next day my husband and mother took me to his office. Mom and the doctor charted our family history of cancer, and it sounded dismal. My mother had been orphaned by the disease. It had killed both her parents and her only sibling, and she had battled cervical and breast cancer since I was in high school. Now it was my turn. The spirit of hopelessness came right into that room and sat next to me on the table. I could feel it put its arm around my shoulder as it whispered, "I've got you now. You're not going to make it; you're going to die. I killed your grandparents, I've tormented your mother, and now I'm going to kill you. No one has been able to stop me!"

The facts were true. This disease had cursed each generation of my family at a younger age. My grandparents were in their fifties, Mom was in her forties, and I was in my late thirties. I was going down.

There were moments in my life when I desperately cried out to God to save me. I knew if he did not answer, I would die. This was one of those moments. I immediately sensed God's presence in the room. His Spirit didn't just sit next to me on that table; he engulfed me, table and all. He cocooned me in a powerful reality as he whispered into my heart, "Don't be afraid, baby girl. I'm right here. Yes, it's true that cancer is in your family tree. Your grandparents could not stand against the cancer. Your mother has stood because of your prayers. She stood because she was under the canopy of your faith, and it was not her time. This is not your time. Give me the diagnosis, and we will do this together. You will stand against this cancer because this is not your time."

I just about slid off the table in complete relief. Once God concluded his visit, I was ready, paper gown and all, to take on cancer with no fear. It wasn't about life being fair or unfair anymore. It was all about glorifying my God. The feelings of helplessness were replaced with empowerment. The doctor released me for forty-eight hours to go home and be with my children, put things in order, and then return for surgery. I faced surgery and did extremely well.

My cancer battle was with advanced stage III breast cancer. My battle was not just about the possibility of losing my life; it was about other real and potential losses that developed along the journey. No one prepared me for some of the losses I suffered: body image, wellness, self-esteem, emotional wellbeing, financial losses, and loss of dreams. The Lord pulled me through those losses to reach the other side of wellness and wellbeing.

Loss of Dreams

The first battle was *the loss of dreams*. I had dreams of the perfect life, of what the future would be. All I had in my hands now were shattered dreams. I didn't like that my future was uncertain, but it was. Would the cancer return? What would the side effects of chemo do to my body? What form of ministry could I do in this fragile state? Those questions were answered the evening of my first operation. After undergoing a modified radical mastectomy that morning, I found it difficult to fall asleep in the hard hospital bed that night. I wasn't at home cuddling with my children, my body hurt, and I was all alone.

As I looked out the window, I began to sink into a state of self-pity. I cried out to God and told him, "I hurt, Lord!" He answered, "Look away from the pain and see things through my eyes." He reminded me of the many women who fight in the big arena of cancer but without the hope and peace I have. God is *not* the person to invite to your pity party! He popped all my pitiful balloons and filled me with his sovereignty as he asked me to read Isaiah 61:1–3.

> The Spirit of the Sovereign Lord is on me,
>   because the Lord has anointed me
>   to preach good news to the poor.

He has sent me to bind up the brokenhearted,
to proclaim freedom for the captives
and release from darkness for the prisoners,
 to proclaim the year of the Lord's favor
and the day of vengeance of our God,
to comfort all who mourn,
and provide for those who grieve in Zion—
to bestow on them a crown of beauty instead of ashes,
the oil of gladness instead of mourning,
and a garment of praise instead of a spirit of despair.
They will be called oaks of righteousness,
a planting of the Lord for the display of his splendor.

The Lord engraved this Scripture on my heart that night.

When I lost the *sense of wellness*, it was shocking, because I didn't know how important it had been to me. I had taken it for granted. There was a loss of feeling safe. I thought my body would always protect me from the elements, but now I found myself a broken person, and I was angry that my body let me down. How dare it get sick like this? I was mad, and I wasn't going to take care of it anymore.

Body Image

Body image has a lot to do with the woman in the mirror, while *self-esteem* is a sense of self-worth and confidence. As I reached the two-month benchmark in my chemo treatments (I would endure six months total), I was twenty-five pounds overweight, all body hair was gone, my head was bald, and about seven faithful lashes were hanging on to each eyelid—all that were left of my full eyelashes. When I looked into the mirror, I saw Mrs. Potato Head looking back at me! She had my green eyes, but nothing else. I couldn't look at my reflection anymore. I used to peek at myself in store windows, but now I was saddened by the image of a pudgy hairless woman in the reflection.

One afternoon while alone at home, I was at the end of what I could endure. As I stood in the bathroom trying to get ready for an appointment, I heard the Lord speak gently to my spirit. He asked me to stop looking at myself through the eyes of the world's system and look at myself through his eyes. He saw an amazing, brilliant, beautifully spirited woman standing in front of him, and he challenged me to stop looking at myself through my eyes and, instead, take a peek at what he sees. He sees into eternity. He sees into the human heart. He sees his purpose being played out in my life. I fell in love with *his* view of me that day, and I chose not to look down or away from myself again. After all, what did I think a warrior looked like? Her hair's not kept, her nails aren't done, and her wardrobe fits tightly for battle. I laugh even now as I think of how I became a poster child that day. Mrs. Potato Head became *Chemo Girl.* My confidence and self-worth were back.

After my treatments ended, I attended a support group where I received insight into my hidden resentment against my body. The counselor instructed us to take an empty chair and place it directly across from where we were seated. I thought it was silly, but I'm respectful of my elders so I placed a chair in front of me. The room was quiet, the lights were low, and I was sitting with my eyes closed. She instructed me to imagine my body, the shell of my skin, lifting off of me and sitting in the other chair, while my spirit and mind remained with me. I have a great imagination so I could see my lifeless shell just sitting there slouching.

The counselor's next words were odd. "Now take a few moments and talk to your body. Tell it what's on your mind." As I looked at my defenseless, broken body I took pity on it. I sensed for the first time in months that it wasn't sick because of neglectful behavior. It was a victim, too! I told my body that I forgave it for getting sick and that I would do my best to take care of it. From that day to this, we've been a good team. After all, a body divided cannot stand.

Cancer is not an inexpensive disease. Medical bills mounted up because I had undergone two hospital surgeries, office visits, chemo treatments, medications, and the loss of employment. I'm thrilled to report that every time I faced financial insecurities, the mailman would come in the nick of time, with cards and letters in his deep pouch. God prompted so many people with the desire to give to my cause; their cards carried emotional support and monetary support as well. God's provision paid the bills, took care of the household budget, and there was even money left over to enjoy ice cream with the children. God countered the financial losses with his amazing provision again and again.

Don't let your situation scare you, whatever it may be. Satan is the one who wants to paralyze you, leaving you ineffective for God's work. Two years after surgery, I became a trained volunteer for the American Cancer Society's Reach To Recovery program, and I made in-home visits to mastectomy patients. I had a choice to make in the spring of 1995: to be an annoyed woman causing people to move away from me, or to be an anointed woman drawing people to the Lord. I'm glad I chose the latter.

Chapter 8

Life After Divorce

Can God Heal a Damaged Legacy?

The church I was attending was part of a denomination that said, "We don't divorce." Women were told to keep the peace and keep praying. No one ever challenged the ungodly behavior of husbands who were unfaithful, abusive, or alcoholic. The elders in the church walked on eggshells around those abrasive, deceitful men. In the past, my dad hadn't stood up for me when Mom's behavior became abusive, and no one had protected me from sexual predators, and now, once again, I found myself in the company of cowards who were not willing to take a stand. I was disappointed and trapped.

When I left my childhood denomination, I saw what the Bible said about my abusive husband, and I slowly found strength to use my voice. When I tried to speak to him about his behavior, it didn't make any difference, and I found myself standing alone. My new church provided protection for the children and me from George and kept us accountable for our attitudes. They warned us if they saw signs of unforgiveness or bitterness creeping into our hearts.

Divorce is not what I wanted, but it's what I was handed in 1998, a year after my second cancer scare and mastectomy. I was on my own with three teenagers, living off my minimum wage. The peace I experienced after getting away from George was priceless. I felt empowered and clearheaded for the first time in my life. For me, the insanity was over, and it was replaced with calm and serenity. But it wasn't that way for my two sons. Tim was thirteen and Kevin was sixteen. They were devastated to hear about the secrets that their dad, their spiritual leader, had kept from them for years. Chrystal was eighteen and her response was totally different. She was relieved because she had been exposed to her father's anger and his embarrassing public behavior. The life we had been living had been anything but normal, and now we all had to find a way to a new healthy normal.

When my husband left his place as the spiritual leader of our home, I felt his protection leave. Prior to his alcoholism, we had felt secure, living under the canopy of his broad shoulders and strong stance. We knew he stood between us and the big mean world, and we were safe. It was devastating when his behavior became unsafe.

God's design for the family is simple but powerful. Wives are to be helpmates to their husbands, and together they're to raise godly offspring. Together we are to advance the kingdom of God forward through our families. But what if you have to do it alone?

Choices

I questioned God about the legacy George had left for my children and their children. Would there be a legacy of a dysfunctional family or the blessing of a family with a healthy future? What was going to be handed down from one generation to the next? What I desired to leave my children would not have material value but great spiritual longevity. I wanted them to know their inheritance in Christ. I wanted to show them the power and fruit of the Spirit that offers eternal life. I asked God if my legacy was damaged. He took my mother's heart to Deuteronomy.

If you fully obey the LORD your God and carefully follow all his commands I give you today, the LORD your God will set you high above all the nations on earth. All these blessings will come upon you and accompany you if you obey the LORD your God (Deuteronomy 28:1–2).

What woman would not like to receive his blessings? Starting in the fall of 1998, I went after those blessings through prayer. Not through poetic or fluffy prayers, but intercessory prayer. Prayer with bite! Prayer with authority! James 5:16 (KJV) says, "The effectual fervent prayer of a righteous man availeth much." Fervent is a loud, large, confident prayer. Who do you think will suffer from this kind of prayer? Satan and his minions will suffer.

I was encouraged when I learned that the child of God has two divine intercessors. Christ intercedes for the believer in heaven, and the Holy Spirit intercedes within the believer on earth.

I had a choice to make. I could either seek God's will or

find answers in the world: money, title, or entertainment (soap operas, movies, and soft porn romance novels). I longed for God's will in my life, because I knew that keeping myself pure today would bring blessings tomorrow. The world was ready to mark my home with the term "dysfunctional family." I had a fight on my hands to not let that title stick to the Davis name.

The courts gave me the title of "displaced homemaker." Because I didn't have a formal education or career and remained home to raise the children, the courts classified me as displaced. George had the education and career training, and now his provision was gone. My heart sank when I heard the term "displaced," but God quickly came to me with this truth, "Patti, you are not displaced. I have you and the children in the palm of my hand. I know right where you are at all times. Hold on to me."

If you're a woman living in today's pressure-cooker world and you're not learning spiritual warfare, you're in trouble. The enemy is taking full advantage of you. Satan would like nothing more than to rob you of your inheritance, separating you from God's strength and power in your life. Ladies, we have to battle *for* our homes, not battle *in* our homes.

Deuteronomy 28 changed my life and my battle plan. Here are a few of the questions I faced. First, would my children turn out all right? How would the rejection of their father affect them? I didn't want to lose all the good work I had put into them.

The fruit of your womb will be blessed (Deuteronomy 28:4).

I've seen God's favor on my children all their lives, and I witness his favor on them still today. A garrison of amazing people came alongside them—teachers and coaches, employers and mentors. God met every one of the personal needs and desires of my children. Every spiritual desire was fulfilled. Each teenager traveled internationally twice on mission trips to places such as Australia, Honduras, and Peru. They never missed a youth retreat. They didn't lack because their heavenly Father's provision filled their lives with activity, and they didn't lack because of a single mother's income.

I could have lost them to rebellion, but God kept them teachable.

I could have lost them to alcohol and drugs, but God kept them joyful and hopeful.

I could have lost them to suicide, but God showed them their talents.

I could have lost them to cults or witchcraft, but God put desires in them to serve and minister.

I could have lost them to laziness, but God stirred them to be hard workers.

I had to fight, through prayer, to keep my blessing. I could never get comfortable. God proved to be a faithful heavenly Father to my children.

> The LORD will grant that the enemies who rise up against you will be defeated before you. They will come at you from one direction but flee from you in seven (Deuteronomy 28:7).

The enemy came in many forms. I had feelings of loneliness and worry. I had to confront the stresses of being the family provider. There was the burden of working while maintaining a home and training children. I was the decision maker in my house, and I still had to care for my health because there were three years left of oral chemo treatments. Not only did God's mighty hand deliver me from each enemy, his hand steadied me. I grew more confident with each victory. My children watched God bring me through, and they chose to make him their God. My legacy was being rebuilt without me knowing it.

> The LORD will send a blessing on your barns and on everything you put your hand to. The LORD your God will bless you in the land he is giving you (Deuteronomy 28:8).

I loved this Scripture because I was able to apply it to all areas of our lives. I would awaken in the night to walk around the house and pray, and I would visit my children while they slept, anoint their heads with oil, and claim the blessing found in this passage. I watched God bless their young lives. When the children came of age they found good jobs, because they had to meet a lot of their own needs. My income was just enough to cover the mortgage and the household budget. Because of God's blessing, whatever we laid our hands to do flourished.

> The LORD will establish you as his holy people, as he promised you on oath, if you keep the commands of the LORD your God and walk in his ways (Deuteronomy 28:9).

I love his title for me and my house: a holy people. Not a dysfunctional family. Others needed to see that we were set apart. We weren't the first family of divorce, and we won't be the last. God made us a light set on the hill, drawing the world toward him. My home was filled with laughter through our countless friends. I taught my children not to be ashamed of the gospel life—to walk it, not just talk it. Do you think for one moment Satan was pleased with us? He hates that we believed in our inheritance, because we became a threat to him. I set my home aside to serve God and let him guide us. Now my children lead their own homes with this same principle. I testify that a family with a past can touch God in the present, a God who is able to change the future! A legacy doesn't just live on. It gets stronger with each generation.

> The Lord will grant you abundant prosperity—in the fruit of your womb, the young of your livestock and the crops of your ground—in the land he swore to your forefathers to give you.

> The Lord will open the heavens, the storehouse of his bounty, to send rain on your land in season and to bless all the work of your hands (Deuteronomy 28:11–12).

A few days before George moved out, I was sitting on the back porch having a conversation with God. "This is really happening, Lord. I'm getting a divorce. I made him leave. What will I do now? My income will be cut by 45 percent. There's no estate to split, no savings to share, and I have nothing in reserve to live off of. No formal education or career to depend on. What am I going to do?"

His answer to me was swift and direct. "I know that you

don't have a storehouse. You don't have a savings account. I'm with you. I will supply you and the children with all your daily needs. When you reach out to me to meet a need, it will be supplied. One day at a time, Patti. I know you don't have a dozen pairs of shoes in your closet, but I promise that I will not let the pair of shoes that are on your feet right now wear out. Walk in faith for your provision. I am with you."

I worked hard to live out an example before my children that God is able to do what he has spoken into our lives. They watched me pick up my manna, God's provisions, every day. Prosperity came in different forms, like appliances that never wore out, cars that kept running, clothes and shoes on clearance. I received promotions at work, and we never went hungry. I was challenged by God to let my children see me stand, believing him while he worked out the details. They rarely saw me fret and become filled with uncertainty. My children saw me pray and then wait on the Lord. My back was up against the wall many, many times. There was nothing more I could do to help myself, so I opened my hands and placed the need in God's huge hands. He never let me walk away from him empty-handed.

The Lord will make you the head, not the tail. If you pay attention to the commands of the Lord your God that I give you this day and carefully follow them, you will always be at the top, never at the bottom (Deuteronomy 28:13).

I had so many questions and concerns about my place and my authority as the head of my home. For several months I harbored a secret question: "Could I, a woman, be enough to hold my post and keep my family together?" I stand only five feet tall, and the world is big and mean, and it wanted to devour my family. I'll never forget how God addressed my fears during a prayer meeting on New Year's Eve, 1999. A good friend came over to me with a word of encouragement. You need to know that I had not shared my concern with anyone. This discerning woman said, "Patti, God is making you a bulwark!" When she spoke those words to me, my spirit sat up and took notice. I felt a surge of strength go down my spine and peace settled instantly over my troubled mind. I must confess I didn't know what the word "bulwark" meant, but I received it to the core of my bones. We found a dictionary to search for the word. I still get goose bumps when I hear the definition: bulwark is "a wall-like defensive structure, a strong support, or protection in danger."

In just one sentence God empowered me for the rest of my life. He was making Patti Davis a strong, wall-like structure in which her children could find support and protection. Wow! Faith is where the battle is won, not in our physical stature. From that night on I never looked over my shoulder again. I kept my face and my attitude turned toward God. Satan wanted me to operate in fear. He wanted me to quit, leave my post, give in, and then finally give up. Then he could have scattered my camp—my family.

Satan has some of you believing it's too late. Your family has been scattered. Your history has already been written. It's a lie! Don't receive it. I want to testify again that a family with a past can touch God in the present, a God who is able to change the future. It can be done. The blessing is ours to reclaim. Claim what is yours in the Lord in spite of your history, in spite of your problems, in spite of your circumstances, and in spite of what others say. Never let the nature of your problems keep you from going to God and asking for a miracle.

God is in the business of reestablishing families and drawing those scattered members back in. Keep praying for your family in obedience and with authority. Create your legacy of a woman who continues to pray. She lets her prayers be strong, large, and bold, and her children will see her God—and their God—be glorified through them.

George and my 10th anniversary photo.

Chapter 9

When Life Hits You Head-On

Life-Changer

I love Fridays! One Friday in August of 2000, my daughter Chrystal and I planned a special evening of dinner and a movie. She picked me up and we were on our way. I love her company so much that I was already having a good time just being in the car with her.

We never made it to the movie that night, because we were involved in a head-on automobile accident a few miles from my home. A nineteen-year-old driver (I later learned that we were the third accident she had on her record) lost control of her car, crossed four lanes of traffic, and struck us, permanently altering our lives.

Our bodies cracked under the pressure of a sixty-mile-per-hour impact. I was knocked unconscious and awoke to the most excruciating pain I'd ever experienced. People were moving in and around our car, offering their assistance. It took forty minutes for the firemen and paramedics to extract us. The pain in my chest was almost unbearable, making it hard to take a breath much less to answer the paramedic's questions. I was afraid that I was dying.

Paramedics discovered damage to my neck, a broken sternum and right hand, and broken kneecaps and right ankle. Several firemen gingerly lifted my injured body from the car and placed me on a backboard. My daughter and I were loaded into the same ambulance because I was very direct with my request to stay close to her. I desperately needed to be as close to my child as possible. I thought I was dying, and I didn't want to die with strangers in the back of a cold, sterile ambulance. I was caught between being a victim and being a mother, and I needed to know my daughter, still my baby girl, was alive and the state of her condition. Wanting to be brave, I pushed through the pain and reassured Chrystal that we were going to make it. But I wasn't sure. We were transported to the hospital and placed in separate rooms.

From the moment I regained consciousness to the moment I was placed on the x-ray table, I'd been crying out to God. The emergency waiting room was filled with family and friends who were also praying, and the church prayer chain had been activated. Numerous people were praying. As I lay on the x-ray table and the imaging machine passed over my broken body, the most amazing thing took place. Peace covered me from my head to my feet. Whatever portion of my body the machine was passing across instantly became warm, and the pain subsided. I felt God's presence in a powerful way. It was as though he was standing at my side passing his hand over my body. The fear of dying lifted off my chest, and I became so calm I could have fallen asleep.

The staff returned me to the emergency room, and my family gathered around me. The doctor announced, with amazement in his voice, that nothing was broken. His words to me were, "Patricia, your x-rays are boring. There's nothing broken." I was still admitted to the hospital for several days due to low blood pressure and the amount of pain I was experiencing. Soft tissue damage is very painful. My body was covered with bruises from head to toe. I rested, enjoyed the painkillers, and looked forward to going home. I was alive, and I wanted to get back to my life.

Life After the Accident

Emergency rooms are designed to deal with trauma. When they don't see blood and guts, they release you and wish you well. As the weeks and months went by, I began to discover just how injured I was. My injuries were deep, severe, and undetected the first days after the accident. For the next twelve months, I coped with serious side effects from the damage done to my body.

Unless your skull is split open, the trauma team doesn't see brain injury. Unless the neck is broken, the trauma team doesn't see severe and debilitating whiplash. Unless bones are broken, the trauma team doesn't see the grave damage done to nerves, cartilage, tendons, ligaments, and muscles. My broken bones were supernaturally healed, but I was left with residual fallout of soft-tissue damage. The damage is permanent, and I'll live with the disabilities until the day I die.

It's bad enough when the doctors don't validate your injuries, and it's twice as agonizing when your auto insurance company won't validate your injuries. I was so naive about insurance companies. I thought they cared about me. I believed that all the premiums I'd paid went for my medical care should I ever need it. I was in for a rude awakening. I struggled to get my insurance company to care for me. It was like pulling teeth to get them to answer me. After getting nowhere with them for eighteen months, I went to see a lawyer, someone to tell me why I wasn't getting help. I went to an auto accident expert.

I know God led me to my attorney, because he championed for me for ten and a half years. My insurance company became the bully, and I needed someone to fight for me. Little did my lawyer and I know the fight would last so many rounds. My case even went before the Colorado Supreme Court. The injustices done to me by the insurance company uncovered a vast array of allegations others have tried to bring against them as well. My case was re-opened and I was awarded lost wages and my medical treatments reinstated.

I keep strict records for the courts and recently counted up some of my doctors' appointments. I was shocked to see that from January 2009 to December of 2012, I had 416 appointments. That's like holding down a part-time job. It's too late for a full recovery from my injuries, however, I spend countless hours in treatments and training to be able to maintain a normal lifestyle.

My team of physicians included a doctor of psychology who helped me cope with the anger and fear caused by the accident. Vision therapy was a non-surgical treatment for problems that interfered with my balance and depth perception as well as reading.

I wouldn't be able to move about as freely as I do today if it weren't for the chiropractic care I receive weekly. A pain management physician treated me for years, and because I live with chronic pain, his approach in easing my suffering has improved my quality of life. There is a tissue that covers all organs of the body and muscles called fascia, and my massage therapist continues to work diligently to release the tension in my fascial system. I wear hearing aids due to the damage of an inner ear concussion, and I live with constant ringing in my ears.

Last but not least, I have a wonderful therapist for mild traumatic brain injury. The brain injury I suffered changed me completely. The damage left me with dyslexia that changes numbers and letters around on me constantly. My short-term memory is severely impaired, and a lack of concentration and confusion plague me daily.

Prior to the accident, I was a productive office manager for a growing, local pest control company. But after three years of not being able to work full time and the countless mistakes I made, I left my job for the sake of the company. The next four years were miserable. I tried to find a stable job with my limited skills, but I had to finally accept the fact that I wasn't going to qualify for a good paying job. I would have to be content with piecing several part-time jobs together. I've worked two and three part-time jobs since the accident, always living from paycheck to paycheck.

I know beyond a shadow of a doubt that God saved my life that evening in August of 2000. He didn't save me so I would be devoured by self-pity and anger. It's unfair what happened to me in that accident, but I'm here to testify that God's grace is sufficient. He asked me to glorify him in all things. I want life to be fair, but it will never be, and God knows it.

You and I will have moments where life hits us head-on, but let's make a resolve that we'll never let go of God's hand. I needed God to heal my broken bones on that x-ray table and to guide me to the wonderful physicians and therapists who made my life manageable again. Every one of them reported my extraordinary attitude of optimism. I didn't get my hope from a prescription bottle. I received it from the Great Physician himself.

My car after the accident.

Chapter 10

Dysfunction And Depression

Codependency

With all the dysfunction in my early life, I developed an un-healthy mindset of loving people in unhealthy ways. Code-pendency is a human condition. It's an unhealthy reliance on people to meet our needs and feed our soul instead of relying on God, and it can cause us to form relationships that are one-sided, emotionally destructive, or abusive. Dependency on destructive people in these broken relationships can make us vulnerable and stunt our growth. It often stems from unhealthy patterns in our family of origin or in significant relationships, and it doesn't develop overnight.

You may be able to relate to my circumstances. The insanity of my life before recovery consisted of physical, emotional, verbal, and sexual abuse. I was in bondage to performance-based love. I was so afraid of rejection that I let other people determine my worth. Remember when I reached bottom at age thirteen? I wanted to die and thought suicide looked like a way out of my pain and the emptiness of my life. Then I had an encounter with God, and I chose life over death. I wish my story ended on that positive note. I wish I could report that the rest of my life went well.

For the next thirty-six years, chaos reigned in my life. Those in my life were not willing or able to fulfill their God-given roles, and I suffered from their lack of protection and leadership. I went from living under the thumb of my angry and depressed mother to being under the thumb of my addicted and abusive husband. Both of them had convinced me my behavior drove their actions of abuse. And I chose to believe them. How sick is that?

This is what codependency looked like in my life:

- Angry people frightened me.
- Personal criticism made me defensive.
- My life was shaped by the demands of the people

around me, and I lost all sense of my own identity.

- I confused love with pity by protecting the addicted or depressed people in my life, rescuing them from their problems.
- I felt responsible for the damaged people in my life and tried hard to help them change their behavior or attitudes.
- I trusted the addicted or depressed person's promises, even if he or she had broken countless promises before.
- I had unhealthy boundaries and couldn't say no without feeling guilty.
- I avoided pain by working, spending, serving, and clowning around—anything to not feel.

When I was thirty-three years old in the summer of 1989, I attended my first workshop on codependency. I learned that I cared too much about what people thought about me. The saddest part was realizing that I based my feelings about me on others' approval. I was afraid of their rejection if I didn't agree with them. Once they knew that my self-esteem depended on their praise, they had me!

In 2006, I made a commitment to walk through a twenty-five-week program called Celebrate Recovery. This program helped me deal with the deep wounds of being the divorced partner of an unfaithful alcoholic. I learned I didn't have to endure the ongoing effects of his limitation, and I didn't have to accept the painful circumstances that his weakness created.

I will always be grateful to God for helping me through my recovery, and for helping me understand the methods of entrapment and dysfunction. He drew me back to his truth about who I am apart from others. I've learned new ways of relating to those around me, to be honest and real with people. Through God's Word, I moved away from focusing on others' needs to focusing on my own sin, my recovery, my life, and my destiny. God taught me then and teaches me now to set healthy boundaries. I remain a caring person, but I'm not a caretaker to everyone. I also learned to stay away from people's verbal reality, which means I don't take abusers at their word anymore—I take them at their behavior. Behavior is always the truth!

I love that God will help us to accomplish freedom from our dependencies and help us move on to build a new life. I saw myself as a warrior, a gifted voice of encouragement to the weak, compassionate and wiser than I ever thought possible. I like feeling brave. An encouraged heart that God occupies is a brave heart that can do battle. It beats being a chicken any day!

I will always be grateful for my Celebrate Recovery group. They were safe women. I was able to share things with them, and they didn't make me feel stupid, nor did they judge me. Because of their acceptance, I felt free to look at my unhealthy patterns, and seek help from others who were also learning to change old habits. One of the hardest things to learn was how to stop playing the blame game. The damage people have done is their responsibility, and what I do with that damage is my responsibility. Offering forgiveness or amends gave me freedom from the lack of peace I felt when I was consumed with hatred, guilt, and shame. Now I run to God with my pain and resentments, my anger and fear. I let the Lord have the last word about me, Patti Davis, a restored woman of God. He has built my ministry to others on the damage of my life that almost destroyed me. The very thing Satan uses to destroy you can be the ministry on which God can build his kingdom.

Hopeless Depression

Persistent heartache and unyielding pressures took over my life in 2005. I could not find four peaceful weeks in a row. Before I recovered from one situation another one was on me. It was overwhelming, and I became depressed. I'd not known heaviness like that before.

"Depression" means hard-pressed. The constant feeling of being pressed down lowered my spirits, which lowered my level of activity and then left me hollow. By November, the mental torment and heartache manifested physically. I was hospitalized with symptoms of a heart attack. I underwent two days of testing and was told that the symptoms were real but tests showed no sign of damage or danger. I was released with a clean bill of health and told to de-stress my life.

Once I was home, I inventoried my life for the past eleven months:

- Struggling financially
- Starting a new job
- Working three part-time jobs
- Beginning menopause
- Seeing youngest child married
- Grieving the empty nest
- Watching the struggle of a child's marriage
- Moving away from my beloved church family for a season
- Dealing with a difficult ex-husband
- Caring for a demanding mother
- Handling major house repairs
- Taking care of minor car repairs
- Preparing for a court trial against my auto insurance company

Somehow I made it through Christmas, but winter was

settling down around me. The nights came earlier, grew darker, and lasted too long. By the end of January 2006, I hit bottom. Each evening as the sun went down, my chest would fill with pressure. I sat in the recliner most of the time because lying down increased the discomfort.

After making several visits to the doctor, I was placed on antidepressants because I told the doctor, "I'm not afraid of dying—I'm afraid of living like this!" I'd totally lost control of my emotions. Menopause had exaggerated my depression. People have always described me as an optimistic person. I found it hard to believe that menopause could strip my sound spirit and leave me in such a tormented state. My motto became, "Menopause sucks . . . the life right out of you!" But I would soon learn that menopause was not the culprit.

In February, when I thought my spirit could not take any more pressure, the heaviness became even heavier, and I went down even more. I experienced a stretch of sleepless nights; I dreaded seeing the sun go down. Before, I would sit out under the moon, but now I hated the night. I didn't sleep for seven nights straight, and I was missing work because of my frail state.

I hated going to bed because it was not a place of rest. It

had become a place of anguish instead. I couldn't get the tension in my chest to subside, and one night I thought I was having a heart attack. But God spoke and reminded me that the cardiologist released me three months earlier with a sound, strong heart. "You're not having a heart attack," the Lord said. I knew instantly the difficulty I was experiencing wasn't physical or emotional. It was spiritual.

I asked God to show me what was causing the chest pains. He answered, "There's a lie stuck in your chest. You don't feel safe being real," he said.

God showed me experiences in my life when I had told significant people about my emotional pain, expecting their support, only to have them back away from me. They would leave me standing all alone, raw and uncovered. I hated that feeling. So I learned from childhood on to be quiet and not say what I really felt. I'd tell them what I thought they wanted to hear. It didn't take long until I started to believe my own superficial expressions. It was still better than feeling alone.

God revealed the profound lie I'd believed: Knowing the truth, standing for the truth, and speaking the truth will leave you standing alone. I had a question for him: "How did you do it? You were crowded in by the multitudes, but you were spiritually alone from childhood to the cross. How did you do it?"

His answer carried a simple but powerful truth: "I was never alone. My Father was with me at all times, and the Holy Spirit was my comfort. My Father and I have never been separated. You have never been separated from us."

My spirit acknowledged this truth. I had another question for God: "What now? How do I get this lie out of my chest?" His response to my problem was gentle and clear-cut. He instructed me to make a list of girlfriends who loved me unconditionally. In just a few minutes I'd constructed a list of thirty-six names. Next he instructed me to call these friends and admit my depression. I was to tell them that I'd not slept in seven nights and that God didn't want me to be alone for the next several weeks. I needed people to spend the night with me and not allow me to be in the house alone. The Lord helped me pick fifteen women who had the spiritual gifts of discernment and service.

The Lord spoke to my spirit, "It may seem like things are falling apart and that you are out of control, but if you will just remain calm, I will lead you out of this place of despair. Don't stand in dread of these things or tremble in fear of what might happen. Rather, cast your cares upon me and recognize that human efforts fall short of my power."

I made the phone calls and confessed to each lady that I didn't know what this was going to look like, but they were picked because of their spiritual gifts. If they had questions about their assignment, they were to go to God for the answers. It was his idea anyway. Each woman picked a date and set her arrival time for the evening. Some brought dinner with them while others arrived just after having dinner with their families.

Not one of those women turned me away or made me feel foolish. It was life changing. Each night I went to my front door and was greeted by a smiling face and a big hug. The women had their overnight bag in one hand and special treats for me in the other. Half of the ladies came dressed in their pajamas. They lavished me with chocolate, cream puffs, flowers, facials, massages, chick flicks, Chinese food, rotisserie chickens, homemade pizza, ice cream, green teas, candles, and praise music! I couldn't wait for the sun to go down each evening because it brought a new indulgence from my friends.

Night after night the dread I'd been living with began to

disappear until it was completely wiped out. The greatest remedy for my depression came from the Scriptures. My girlfriends went before the Lord on my behalf and then wrote down what the Lord told them. No one knew how bad it had been for me. No one knew the deep questions I'd been wrestling with. Satan had me thinking I'd done something wrong. God gave me just enough strength to step away from the lie and step into his presence, and then I stepped up to hear his Word through those ladies.

The Healing Words of Friends

I kept a journal of some of the Scriptures and prophetic words that brought instant restoration to my broken heart. My friends spoke to me of God's delight in me and of his love—love that held me even when I didn't believe it. He already knew of my weariness and sorrows, and instead of burying my grief, I was to offer it up to him. He would lift every one of my burdens. They invited me to listen to his heartbeat instead of the enemy's lies, and they reminded me that "sorrow lasts for a night, but joy comes in the morning" (Psalm 30:5, my paraphrase). And Psalm 71:20–21:

Though you have made me see troubles, many and bitter, you will restore my life again; from the depths of the earth you will again bring me up. You will increase my honor and comfort me once again.

They encouraged me to replace old patterns with the true intimacy of God's love, and to see my depression as an "emptying out." The old vessel was being completely emptied to make room now for something new. This was not hitting bottom; this was an emptying out. Not destruction, but renewal, restoration, and regeneration. All the old must go, every drop, so that God can begin to fill me with new wine. None of the old can remain. Not my pain or my distrust of people or my sorrow—it must all go!

They showed me that my family was under God's watchful eye, and just like Job, the latter part of my life may be more blessed than the first part (Job 42:12). They gave me Scriptures that spoke of protection and peace.

> Do not touch my anointed ones; do my prophets no harm (Psalm 105:15).

> I will lie down and sleep in peace, for you alone, O Lord, make me dwell in safety (Psalm 4:8).

And another that told of God's strength when I am weak:

> Whom have I in heaven but you?

And earth has nothing I desire besides you.
My flesh and my heart may fail,
but God is the strength of my heart and my portion forever.
Those who are far from you will perish;
you destroy all who are unfaithful to you.
But as for me, it is good to be near God.
I have made the sovereign Lord my refuge;
I will tell of all your deeds (Psalm 73:25–28).

I stand in awe when I think of how God broke through the lies with his prophetic words and Scriptures. Only the Holy Spirit could have told my girlfriends what to say. I admitted my fear and risked being real with the friends God had picked for me, and I was not left standing alone. I was tenderly protected by those friends until I could find my way out of the dark oppression.

I learned a lesson and found a new respect for people suffering from depression. I learned that oppression might be from the enemy. Too many times I've given people pat answers like "just pray more, claim your Scriptures, and fill your home with praise music." I gave them those answers because I didn't know what to do or I didn't have the time to see them through that dark season. Sometimes I even judged them for being weak. God showed me how to rise up and defeat the enemy of my soul. Now I know how to minister to people struggling with depression. I will never again give them a quick answer. I'll give them my testimony instead. I'll encourage them to find out what lie is stuck in their chest.

I can't tell you how it happens, but I know that when my weak heart comes in contact with God's strong heart, I gain strength. I can't tell you how it is that I'm able to receive into my spirit his power to do and bear all things. But, by communion with God, it is possible. Friend, we won't make it if we don't step into his will and step away from the will of our flesh.

Sometimes the pressure we feel is God taking us through the wine press. He pressed the bitterness out of me and filled me with an aromatic wine that refreshes the people who cross my path. God took the hopelessness out of my depression.

Chapter 11

Second Chance, Second Divorce

Second Marriage

I described my debilitating depression to you in the last chapter and how with the help of friends I came out of that dark place of oppression. As I was returning to a state of stability, I received a surprising phone call one morning. It was my exhusband asking for my forgiveness. He told me humbly that he was sorry for all the heartache he had caused for all those years.

He, too, had been wrestling for the past year with debilitating depression that took him to the end of his alcoholism. While I was home being emptied out, he sat in his apartment, bottoming out. He wasn't attending church; he'd driven everyone away, and he was losing his job of eighteen years because he'd been caught intoxicated at work. He called me to ask for help out of his pit.

I wasn't caught off guard by his phone call because God had been preparing me for it. During the months of my depression I found myself crying out to God on George's behalf. I knew he'd trashed his life and was isolated from everyone, and without God's help, he would be one tormented man. I had compassion on him, prayed for him, and asked God to save his soul.

There he was, on the other end of the phone asking, "Is there any hope for us? Even for a friendship? Is there any hope, Patti?" Because I'd been brought through my process of healing, I was able to answer yes to the friendship. If God had not emptied me of all distrust, I would have never been able to receive George's request that day.

A few days later I went to his apartment, and with help from neighbors, drove him to the hospital. Our daughter Chrystal met us at the emergency room. After three days in detox, he was accepted into a rehab facility and began his twenty-eight-day program. George had never asked for help like this, and we were hopeful for him.

We corresponded through letters; his honesty in them was a welcome change for me. As the days grew into weeks, I grew to be quite comfortable around him, and a friendship developed between us. We had plenty to talk about when we were together, and it was nice to not feel alone. The weeks grew to months.

I went before the Lord to ask, "Where is this going? Are you doing a miracle of reconciliation? How do I pray, Lord? Do I say *him* or do I say *us*?" I felt the Lord tell me to pray for *us* as a couple. George presented himself as a changed man. He was attending recovery classes, Alcoholics Anonymous, and church. We were going to counseling together and moving toward the possibility of marriage. And he'd found a new job, better than the job he had lost earlier. All the signs looked good.

There was one phrase George kept saying that brought relief to my weary soul. As I juggled my finances, he would tell me to stop trying to do it alone, stop trying to carry the load alone, because he was now there to help me. I loved hearing those words. I could feel the weight lift off my shoulders each time he said that to me. It was nice to have help.

Nine months into our reconciliation, I accepted his proposal for marriage. We remarried on our thirtieth wedding anniversary with our children at our sides, and my mother and two hundred guests in attendance. We came back together like ducks taking to water and didn't miss a step. Our home was filled with Bible studies, friends, grandchildren, and lots of laughter.

It was exciting to watch George get his life back. People who had known him from the past couldn't believe the change they saw in him. They noticed how alive he looked and how his eyes shone again. His humbleness and his willingness to be accountable brought me security, and I looked forward to the rest of our lives.

Second Divorce

To my deep disappointment, familiar traits began to appear just six months into our new marriage. George started using alcohol again. I was totally blindsided. He was shocked by the setback as well, so I let grace cover the first offense. He promised to do better, but to no avail. For the next eighteen months, his addiction took a devastating toll on our relationship, my physical safety, and my sanity. The drinking didn't stop, and the hiding began. George lived in two completely different worlds, and he worked hard to keep his worlds separate. I was caught in the collision of those two worlds.

He drank eighteen of the twenty-four months of the marriage. He was fired from four jobs for coming to work drunk or missing work because he was drunk. Finally he just stopped looking for work and sat in front of the television while I worked three jobs. Each month brought more verbal abuse, and he developed a total disregard for my physical and emotional wellbeing. He walked away from every source of counseling that held him accountable.

A damaging blow to my frayed spirit came in June of 2007. A few days after George was released from detox again, the police came to our home because my daughter and friends were afraid he would kill me. This was the second time. The final dispatch of officers sent me straight to counseling. The counseling group reminded me that I didn't cause his addiction and I couldn't cure it, no matter how supportive and attentive I was.

I had to protect myself from his bad choices. Again I found my voice and stood up to George. My best care-giving efforts weren't going to remedy his problem. The more he drank, the more he fueled his nasty characteristics of rebellion and control, anger and resentment. Then came the onslaught of justification and lack of accountability, selfishness and pride. It sickened me to see him jeopardize his morals, values, family, relationship, and job again, all the while rationalizing his behavior. As he gave up all his dignity; I lost all my respect for him.

By our second wedding anniversary, I'd placed him on a plane to a rehab facility out of state. I needed to get him as far away from me as possible, so I could feel safe from his dangerous behavior and start focusing on saving my life, my sanity, and my spirit.

George's addictions had once again consumed my life, my finances, my friendships, and my health. I was at the lowest point of my life. When I had remarried George, I had refinanced my home and paid off eighteen thousand dollars of his medical bills so we could start with a clean slate. He was forgiven his debt. But now, due to his unemployment and new medical bills, my savings were drained, and an avalanche of debt of over one hundred thousand dollars buried me. This did not include the foreclosure of my home. I couldn't believe how he had wiped me out in just eighteen months. George had presented himself as a changed man, and my need to ease the pain of loneliness made it seem worth the risk. I truly thought we would make it.

It all ended in a second divorce. He never acknowledged what he did, apologized, offered any financial support, or sought help to change his ways. When I lost my house and I locked the front door for the last time on September 28, 2008, I began a thirty-month journey through the wasteland of homelessness.

Chapter 12

Homeless

Air Mattresses, Soft Beds, and Firm Futons

I learned the definition of *homeless* while working in the office of a public school years earlier. The school documented students as homeless if their families were living with relatives or in a friend's home as a temporary solution because they could not afford their own place. You are considered homeless if you don't possess a permanent mailing address. I thought homeless only applied to those who had been without a roof for a certain period of time and lived in cardboard boxes, tents, or shelters.

In September of 2008, I went on record as being homeless, totally dependent on the generosity of family and friends.

For the next thirty-two months I would move ten times. If I'd known the struggles ahead of time, it would've pushed me over the edge for sure! God put a strong resolve in my spirit to take life one day at a time, all 972 days of them.

I cried a lot the first four months, several times during the day and every night while alone in a strange bed. As I drove the streets looking for work, desperately looking for a way to survive, I often became overwhelmed with grief and had to pull the car over to the side of the road. I truly thought the waves of sorrow would sweep my car away. God's presence kept me anchored enough to not be swept away under more than I could endure.

I lost my home of the past fifteen years because of the destructive and costly behavior of George. For the next twelve months, he was safe in rehab as I wandered through the wasteland of homelessness. I had five different addresses. My mail became so tangled in the numerous forwarding changes that my mother allowed me to receive mail at her home.

I was grateful for the amazing people who heard about my plight and opened up a room for me in their home. This gratitude carried me for a while, but as time dragged on, my spirit began to show signs of wear and tear. I'd been the alpha female running my own home for thirty-two years, and now the role of always being a guest in someone else's home was wearing on me. Even though I was grateful, it was hard to be confined to a small portion of a house sleeping on air mattresses, soft beds, and firm futons.

The economic recession was devastating for me as well as many others and made work almost impossible to find. I had to sell all my possessions to have money to live on. Every piece of furniture every curtain, every knick-knack, and even my dinnerware were sold. I could only keep the items that would fit in my car. I couldn't part with the sentimental gifts and keepsakes from my children's childhood, so I stored about sixty boxes of precious items in the smallest storage unit I could afford. All I really had left was *me*.

An agonizing reality hit me the first time one of my children came home to Colorado for a visit—I had no home for them. We struggled through the heartache together as we faced the fact that their home was gone. I died inside when I wasn't able to offer them a bed to sleep in. They had to make arrangements with my mother or friends who lived in town. I hated it!

My heart ached as I realized that their childhood home filled with memories of their adolescence was gone. The backyard that hosted graduation parties, Chrystal's bridal shower, and Kevin's bachelor party was gone. The grandchildren had had their birthday parties and sleepovers in my home, but now we were forced to make arrangements to meet somewhere else.

By March of 2009, I had become so discouraged that the oppressiveness of being homeless was becoming almost too much to bear. Satan was doing his best to make me feel responsible for everything that had happened and tried to seduce me into taking the blame for others' actions. He's the accuser and was set on bringing serious accusation against me, this time from the past. I'd received a hurtful letter from a family member filled with resentment toward me and my situation. I went running to God with the pain, and his answer to me was perfect.

The Lord said, "Resist. If you succumb to this seduction, it will take you out of the flow of the Spirit and will dump you down into the flesh. Resist, Patti. Old issues that have been out of sight and out of mind are coming up for review. Dealing with these things will not necessarily be comfortable or fun.

But, it can be profitable if you rise above emotionally charged memories to a higher perspective to look through the eyes of the Spirit instead of looking through the eyes of the flesh. This is a time when you will come to a great and lasting resolution once and for all."

I wanted to arrive at that great and lasting resolution *yesterday*! For weeks I'd been saying to myself, "I don't mind dying right now." I wasn't suicidal, but if death had met me on the street, I would have welcomed it. I was tired of the situation and wanted to go to sleep and not wake up.

A Friend's Words

It would take a few more days before the Lord broke through my discouragement with a wonderful vision. The vision came through the love and wisdom of a new friend I'd made. I told him about the feelings of darkness, loneliness, pressure, and the fearless yearning for death. He asked me a funny question.

"Patti, what is your favorite fruit?"

I told him it had to be something red like strawberries or cherries.

He replied, "Okay, you're a cherry tree."

I envisioned a cherry tree as he spoke to me about how grand my tree was to those around me. My fruit and my shade brought pleasure to many lives. But he also mentioned that my cherry tree had weathered more than its share of storms in life. Now I saw the broken but mended branches of that tree. I saw where fools had carved their profanity into its bark. It was a totally functioning tree, just not the perfect tree God had designed.

I questioned if the discouragement I felt was because God was about to prune my tree more. But God answered, "No, this is not a season of pruning." Next, I thought about the tree that didn't bear much fruit in the Bible, and I asked God if he was going to cut me down to a stump and let me grow from new saplings. But God answered, "No, I'm not going to grow anything new from the old portions of your tree." So I asked God what was to become of me.

My friend asked me another question. "Patti, look closely at the cherry—what lies deep inside of it?"

I was quiet, and then he answered for me. "The seed. Your seed, *your destiny*! Your destiny has not changed nor has it altered in any form, no matter what has happened to your life." I saw my seed fall to the ground, be buried by the soil, and lie dormant until new life sprouted from it. At that moment, I understood that the darkness surrounding me was not evil, but was necessary to germinate the seed. I understood that the loneliness and pressure was not from abandonment, but from God setting me apart. The yearning for death was not a destructive death, but a death needed for a resurrection. New life from a fresh, new source—not sprouting from the old tree trunk. Jesus said in John 12:24:

> I tell you the truth, unless a kernel of wheat falls to the ground and dies, it remains only a single seed. But if it dies, it produces many seeds.

The discouragement lifted and was replaced with patience as I remained steadfast and faithful. The Lord showed me it was more important than ever for me to persevere. I'd still be tested with temptations to be disappointed and become discouraged, but I could not give up. I kept pressing through, and I felt God with me. It wasn't an easy time, but I believed he would bring me into victory at some point. He'd done it so many times before. Why would he leave me now?

The Lord Breaks Through

By June of 2010, I'd moved three more times. Each move, my

mother made the generous offer for me to live with her. She was still living in my childhood home, all nine hundred square feet of it. I always cringed and made an excuse to not go home. She didn't get it—I hated that house. It was hard enough to visit that place, much less think of ever living there. But God had other plans, and through a series of events I landed back at my mother's home. It was the last place on earth I wanted to be, but there I was. She bought a futon and placed me in the room that used to be Daddy's man cave.

I felt I could handle it because I was working three part-time jobs and had my activities with friends. Just like in my childhood, I could avoid being home through the excuse of work and activities. Mom's health was failing and knowing she wasn't alone brought her and my siblings comfort. I submitted to the situation and took up residency as my mother's cook, housekeeper, and taxi driver, and we filled the house with my friends and lots of laughter.

It only took two days for the tormenting spirits to find me in my childhood home. Bad dreams, headaches, and abdominal pain started to plague me when I was alone in that bedroom. After enduring the attack for three days, I found myself standing in the hallway crying out to God. My desperate words to him were: "God, please. Do I really have to be here? I hate this house. That room is a place of torment for me!" Just as I spoke the words "that room," I realized I was sleeping in my old bedroom. I had left that room at age twenty and planned never to return. Now I had to make my bed in there again. "Oh God, I don't want to be here."

In an instant that despairing hallway became a portal to heaven, and God himself came down to be with me. He placed his hand on my shoulder and, in the Spirit, showed me some powerful truths.

"Yes, that's your childhood bedroom, but do you remember what took place between you and me in that room?"

I answered, "Oh, yes! You came to me when I was thirteen years old! You sat on my bed, and you saved my life from my plan of suicide!"

"Yes, I did," the Lord said. "Patti, wherever I place my feet is holy ground. Your bedroom is *not* a room of torment, it is holy ground. That's where it all began for you and me." I smiled and asked God if he was going to come and sit on my bed more often now.

Then the Lord gave me a vision of something else. He reminded me that when I was thirteen years old, I had built an altar in remembrance of what he had done for me. Then he helped me see in the vision that the altar was still standing after all those years. He told me to look for it. It was in the room, but years of weeds had grown up around it and hid it from plain view. When I spotted it, He instructed me to brush away the vines and read the words engraved on its side. I was awestruck as I read these precious words from Jeremiah 29:11:

> For I know the plans I have for you, declares the LORD, plans to prosper you and not harm you, plans to give you hope and a future.

God had been preparing me for several months prior to this incident. My devotionals had conveyed a message of hope that showed me God was going to let me cross over into the Promised Land soon. My time in the wilderness was coming to an end, and I was anticipating that event.

God asked me another question, "Patti, how old were you when I came to you?"

"I was thirteen years old, Lord."

"How old are you now?" He asked.

"I'm fifty-three years old, Lord."

Then I smiled as I did the math. Forty years! I had been wandering in the wilderness for forty years. Not because of my disobedience, but because I was the child of a disobedient older generation. I had no idea that I was going to cross over to the Promised Land through my childhood bedroom. I had imagined a more angelic setting for the crossover. But, God is God, and his ways are not my ways.

When God was done with me in the hallway, I was ready to face my futon with new resolve. I was now sleeping on holy ground, and it doesn't get better than that here on earth. I remained with my mother for eleven months. She passed away just six weeks after I moved out and into my own apartment. I made sure I was just minutes from her in case she needed me. Before she died, she was able to visit my new home and was pleased and happy for me.

My homelessness taught me a powerful truth through all of God's spoken words to me. "You have been crushed and stomped and broken, but I tell you that you are becoming vintage wine. You will be my broken bread and poured-out wine that I give to those around you. Do not despair. Rise up in faith that I will use you."

The world used me and I was left broken. God uses me, and I'm left enlarged and revived. What a mystery!

Chapter 13

My Children, My Choices

I was twenty-four years old when I gave birth to my first child in 1980. It seems funny now, but people then believed I had started my family late at age twenty-four. My school friends had all married right out of high school and began having their babies by age nineteen. Oh, how our society has changed! But I know that my babies came at just the right time for me. I loved being pregnant, and my labor was easy. I was the woman every other woman in labor hates. My first child was delivered in four and a half hours; the second baby took two hours, and the third little fellow would have been a sneeze but he came "sunny side up," so it took another hour to deliver him.

My Vow to Be a Good Mother

In the previous chapters, I shared with you how important it was for me to be a good mom. It's a decision I made while still a young girl—not as a reaction against my mother's example, but because of the excellent example of my grandmother, her friends, and the ladies in the church. With the help of the Holy Spirit, I was guided through the journey of motherhood. I was a good mother—not perfect, but a woman who asked God for instructions, knowing he had given her a mother's heart.

My first priority as a mother was to be a safe person who was predictable and someone my children knew would protect them from danger, both physically and spiritually. They heard me often pray protection over them. I wanted more than anything for my children to be able to trust me and to know they could reach out to me and depend on me. God helped me create a home where my children were not in bondage to panic or anxiety, unable to love or learn.

I wanted to be a cheerleader for my children, someone who was really excited about them and their talents. I wanted my children to hear their mother cheering them on, even if I was off in the distance, as they were engaged in an activity about which they were passionate. My mother had always been jealous of me, and to get a compliment out of her was like pulling teeth. Praise would not come from her mouth, so I learned to ask yes or no questions like "Did you like what I just made?" I hoped her answer would be "yes." I'm so thankful to God that he helped me turn the table on my bad experiences. He filled my neglected heart with a supernatural, unselfish love for my children.

As I write this, I can visualize where I was when I made that silent vow to myself to be a good mother. I was in junior high and my Sunday school teacher was a gentleman named Mr. Eddie. Our class was located in the balcony of the sanctuary. One Sunday Mr. Eddie passed out small pieces of paper around the class and instructed us to write down what we wanted to be when we grew up. The class remained quiet as we all thought about his question and then wrote down our answer. We passed our papers to the front, and after Mr. Eddie collected them, he began to read them off. No one wrote their names on the papers; we just wrote down our dreams. I remember feeling embarrassed as I heard what the others had written down. Several of my peers wanted to be missionaries, while others wanted to be doctors or teachers. But I had passionately written, "I want to be a Christian mother." God heard Patti Wells make that vow, and he enveloped my desire with his love and power.

My Children

Chrystal was my firstborn and a precious little girl. She had a head of black hair and the longest eyelashes I'd ever seen. Her eyes were very big and brown; they looked like two large chocolate chips resting on a bed of cream cheese. I remember asking her daddy, "How are we ever going to discipline her with those big eyes?" His answer to me was, "She'll have to wear sunglasses all of her life." I was pleasantly surprised by my ability to lavish love on her and then later on her brothers—it came as naturally as breathing. I now know that was a gift from God. Chrystal had the sweetest temperament and continues to be a sweetheart to everyone who crosses her path. She has a silent strength and a level of endurance that never ceases to amaze me. I want to be like her when I grow up.

Kevin, our first boy, came second. We called him our little mouse because he was petite like Chrystal. I giggled at his tiny legs because they looked like they belonged to an old man. But as Kevin grew, those little legs turned into legs of steel. He has an outward strength that is obvious to anyone who meets him, and I always feel secure whenever he's standing close. As a child, he was full of animated inquisitiveness. He could get us to laugh at things that should have unraveled us. To this day he's able to laugh at himself when he's put himself in a frustrating position.

Timothy was the last baby I would have, but he was far from the least. He came in as our heavyweight, looking like a German dumpling. At birth his chest measured fourteen inches around. I'd given birth to a giant! I needed a tow truck to carry him around; I only stand five feet tall, while my ex-husband stands five feet, eleven inches. Somewhere in our genetic engineering we wired Tim to grow to the adult height of only five feet, four inches. Many people have tried to size up Tim by his outward appearance only to discover the giant that lives within him. He has a quiet strength and a compassionate spirit that benefits us all. He is a champion.

All three of my children, their spouses, and my grandchildren have a great sense of humor. One of my greatest joys is knowing they all love and fear God. They love life, and they all watch out for each other. They don't go around demanding of life; instead, they look for opportunities where they can make a difference in the lives around them.

Choices

On September 13, 1980, I had a choice to make: either I could regurgitate the things done to me from my childhood onto my children, or I could stand up and stop the insanity with this new generation. The temptation to be short-tempered and sarcastic came often, but God was right there to empower me to resist and not hurt my children.

I want to encourage you again that if there were wrongs done to you, God can help you change patterns and habits of behavior and begin to put things right. I truly believe that God gave my mother and father a second chance through their grandchildren. My parents were awesome grandparents to the ten babies my siblings and I gave them. They were right there when each one was born; they never missed a birthday party, and they said yes to every invitation for school programs or sporting events. When Mom and Dad passed away, the grand-children took turns at the funeral services reflecting about their relationships with their grandparents.

I enjoyed seeing my mom's and my dad's playful side with the children. I set a silent standard that said my children would be respected, appreciated, and showered with the words "I love you." I never worried about my parents harming them. What a nice healing for us all. There were times when I felt jealous of my children, and I thought how nice it would have been to be their grandchild instead of their child. The hugs and laughter my children showered on both my parents was very healing.

Chapter 14

The Healing Journey

Inside my Bible cover are written these words: *God does not promise a comfortable journey, only a safe landing.*

I love those words. If you're reading this, then you've stayed with me all the way to my last chapter. Women ask me all the time about the healing journey and where to start for themselves. Let's talk about that for a moment.

Spiritual Maturity

When you look up the word "healing" in the dictionary, it means *to restore health; make well; cure.* The word "journey" means *going to a place; a distance.* It's safe to say that any journey that covers a distance is going to take awhile. So pack a lunch because our journey is toward spiritual maturity, it's going to take awhile, and there are no shortcuts. Believe me, I have spent fifty-six years looking for the shortcuts! What I found instead were many examples in the Bible of people who had safe landings even though their journey was anything but comfortable. Noah, Joseph, Moses, Ruth, Esther, and Job are just a few. Their lives give a realistic portrait of life with its struggles and tragedies, yet also reveal how the faith and faithfulness of godly people enable God to turn tragedy into triumph and defeat into redemption.

I love the word "redemption" because inside of that word I find rescue and deliverance, release and restoration. To someone like me who lived in bondage, slavery, and brokenness, these are lovely words. When you and I experience adversity on our journey through earth, it becomes God's opportunity to advance his great purpose in and for your spiritual maturity. I encourage you to take on the attitude of Moses in Deuteronomy 2:7.

He [God] has watched over your journey through this vast desert. These forty years the LORD your God has been with you, and you have not lacked anything.

I set out on a journey to become a Christian mother, and it

took forty years. There were no shortcuts.

You've just finished reading about my journey in the previous chapters. Now I have grandchildren who pray for me in their nighttime prayers. It wasn't always a comfortable journey, but by the grace of God I experienced a safe landing. The book of Numbers reveals the profound principle that if one generation fails God, he will raise up another one to fulfill his promises and carry out his mission.

If you and I need a healing, then something is broken. When something is bringing us discomfort and pain, how do we deal with it? We take that complaint to the doctor and inform him that we feel disjointed or something hurts. The doctor orders an x-ray.

Under God's Light

First, God is going to ask you to hold yourself up to his light. We can't guess what might be wrong because we need an x-ray to penetrate our flesh and illuminate the source of our pain that is lodged deep inside. The Holy Spirit will penetrate your soul and illuminate the source of your pain, whether it's self-inflicted or an injury. God's illumination will tell us what's wrong.

Ask yourself: Am I ...

- Resentful. Am I holding a grudge?
- Self-absorbed. Am I being selfish?
- Anxious. Am I full of worry?
- Complacent. Am I passive?
- Unrealistic. Am I denying reality by ignoring problems and hoping they'll go away?
- Self-indulgent. Have I become impulsive?

This is the message we have heard from him and declare to you: God is light; in him there is no darkness at all. If we claim to have fellowship with him and yet walk in the darkness, we lie and do not live by the truth. But if we walk in the light, as he is in the light, we have fellowship with one another, and the blood of Jesus, his Son, purifies us from all sin. If we claim to be without sin, we deceive ourselves and the truth is not in us. If we confess our sins, he is faithful and just and will forgive us our sins and purify us from all unrighteousness. If we claim we have not sinned, we make him out to be a liar and his word has no place in our lives (1 John 1:5–10).

When I became a cancer patient, I needed to submit to the doctors who specialized in the illness. After finding a lump, the family doctor told me to get a mammogram. The radiologist told me to see a surgeon. The surgeon said that the breast needed to be removed. The pathologist said it was time to see the oncologist. The oncologist said the ugly word, *chemo*. To save my life, I submitted to their treatment plan for five years.

Now, I must have a cancer checkup once a year for the rest of my life.

Submission is a tough pill to swallow, but there are blessings that cannot be obtained if we cannot accept, submit, and endure suffering. Because I submitted to the doctors' advice and endured the suffering, I've had the privilege of watching my three children graduate from high school, I danced at their weddings, and I was there when they held their newborn babies.

When I became a single mother of three teenagers, I needed to submit to God as the authority in my home. The world said I had the right to be angry, depressed, resentful, and vindictive toward my ex-husband. But God asked me to keep my face and my attitude turned toward him, and he would get my family through that sad and terrible time. I was about to travel through a big, mean world that loves to devour single-parent families and ravage children.

Because I accepted and endured the heartache of abandonment years ago, today I enjoy seeing all three of my adult children in ministry and service to their communities. They have learned about the father-heart of God and are raising my grandchildren to love and fear the Lord. Who would have thought that healing lies in the ability to submit?

Job is a great biblical example. His final answer to God was one of absolute humility and submission to his newfound revelation.

"I know that you can do all things; no plan of yours can be thwarted" (Job 42:1).

I witnessed the alcoholic who wouldn't admit he had a problem until he lost his family, friends, health, and job. Unacknowledged sin is like cancer cells. If it's caught at an early stage of growth, through regular checkups, the prognosis is good. But if it's left to grow undetected, the prognosis is bad or even deadly. Living in the Lord's light and holding ourselves accountable to God on a daily basis prevents major spiritual crises.

God wants to show you aspects of your life you have not considered. He wants to reveal things so that you can see yourself in the light of truth. He saw the situations I was in, and he saw rejection, offense, guilt, and shame.

Help means the Holy Spirit takes hold of me and my weaknesses instead of leaving me on my own. " . . . the Spirit helps us in our weakness" (Romans 8:26). God has joined me in every situation life has thrown at me to help empower me to be a conqueror instead of a victim of my circumstances. When we are helpless, the Holy Spirit is truly our helper. Don't be afraid to look closely at your heart today. He won't be able to heal what you don't acknowledge and confess. Call your pain and frustration by its name; hold it up to God's light and let him shine his truth on that hurtful spot.

Trust the Outcome

Second, when we have a medical treatment plan, we have to trust the outcome to the professionals. In the same way that we need to trust our doctors, we also need to trust God. Everything that God permits he does so in wisdom and with purpose. Even the suffering of the righteous has meaning and divine purpose.

Isaiah 53:5 says, "by his wounds we are healed." I respect the work Jesus did for me at Calvary, and I do not take it for granted. I'm at a loss for words when I think about the beating he took. Jesus bore *all* our pain caused by the evil in another human heart. Too many times we refer to only the wounds of a diseased or broken body. But those injuries only affect the tissues of our body. What about the issues of our hearts and emotions? The Roman soldier who beat Jesus represents the people in our lives who have beaten us with verbal, sexual, or physical instruments, and broken our spirits.

During his beating and on the cross, Jesus took upon himself every level of personal violation any human could ever inflict upon another. Every human depravity was laid upon his beautiful, blameless back. When they were done beating him, his flesh was far more than just bruised. It was torn, and it hung in chunks from his back and his sides.

That Roman soldier came at Jesus just like your abuser comes at you, with mental depravity, evil intention, and demonic forces to kill your spirit, and perhaps your body. Believe me when I say there is nothing you can't bring to Jesus that he has not personally experienced. And when you bring it to him you will hear him say, "Yes, I know exactly how you feel. I felt that rip into my flesh, too. Now let my Spirit heal you. Not at a superficial level, but to the deepest level. My Spirit can go to the core of your heart and lift the stain of pain out and carry it far away from you."

Jesus is our perfect example of submission because he submitted to the will of his Father God.

> If you have any encouragement from being united with Christ, if any comfort from his love, if any common sharing in the Spirit, if any tenderness and compassion, then

make my joy complete by being like-minded, having the same love, being one in spirit and purpose. Do nothing out of selfish ambition or vain conceit, but in humility consider others better than yourselves. Each of you should look not only to your own interests, but also to the interests of the others. Your attitude should be the same as that of Christ Jesus:

Who, being in very nature God, did not consider equality with God something to be grasped, but made himself nothing, taking the very nature of a servant, being made in human likeness. And being found in appearance as a man, he humbled himself and became obedient to death—even death on a cross!

Therefore God exalted him to the highest place and gave him the name that is above every name, that at the name of Jesus every knee should bow, in heaven and on earth and under the earth, and every tongue confess that Jesus Christ is Lord, to the glory of God the Father (Philippians 2:1–11).

To be made nothing is a phrase used in the Greek. It literally means he emptied himself as one would pour out and entirely empty the contents of a glass.

Jesus voluntarily emptied himself of his heavenly glory, passions, eternal riches, rights, and the uses of divine attributes. Jesus, who is without sin, also took on our fully human nature with its temptations, humiliations, and weaknesses. He also took on our human limitations, sufferings, misunderstandings, ill treatment, and hatred. He bore all these things by taking on the curse of death on the cross. Through Jesus' work on the cross, I get to trade my despair and my terror, my depression and my humiliation, my weeping and my unceasing grief, and I get to pick up his prescription for peace, comfort, relief, and help. It's a wonderful trade, isn't it?

Peace

In John 16:33, Jesus said, "In this world you will have trouble." If Jesus says it's going to happen, count on it. But he also said he would give us his special brand of *peace*. The world's peace only comes when circumstances are easy. I've experienced God's peace when all hell was breaking loose. It was a peace that overcame anxiety and fear even when everyone else around me became overwhelmed. The Apostle Paul prayed three times that his physical infirmities would leave him. God sometimes sees fit to sacrifice our temporary pleasure, health, or even prosperity in order to do a deeper, more important work in our hearts.

God gives us his peace that comes from the nearness of his presence. I've had to lie down in some uncomfortable, oppressive places. But God's presence was over and around me when:

I lay there with a broken heart in a defiled marriage bed.

I lay there with a broken spirit from verbal abuse, humiliation, and rejection.

I lay there with a broken body from physical and sexual abuse, cancer, and a crushing auto accident.

I testify that the bed I found myself lying in was always placed right in the center of his large hand, and God gave me his peace that truly does come from the nearness of his presence.

Forgiveness

The next big question I'm always asked is, when will my healing be complete? I asked God this question, and I felt he told me that healing is complete when we truly have been able to *forgive*. Just like doctors order another x-ray to see if what had been disjointed now lines up or orders another blood test to see if blood is now free from impurities. Let's run tests on our hearts.

The test for forgiveness is important in knowing that my healing is complete. The word "forgive" appears over 140 times in the New Testament. It means *to let go; to leave behind; to dismiss; and to cancel a debt.* It's used for the forgiveness of sins by God. He cancels our guilt. We are to forgive others who do us wrong in the same way God forgave us. So within the healing process, we must be prepared to forgive!

I noticed that there was a mental torment of unforgiveness in me. If a selfish person has bruised your heart, you must forgive that person in order to protect yourself from Satan's mental oppression. If Jesus can forgive his murderers—then I, his daughter, can forgive people in my life. God is not asking us to forgive. He commands us to forgive.

I used to have an excuse for not being able to forgive, and I thought it was a good one. I told God I was in too much pain to forgive, but God responded with one of Jesus' last recorded acts of ministry: He forgave the thief hanging next to him on the cross and those who had hung him on that cross.

I don't want unforgiveness to separate you from God. You need him too much. Forgiveness is a choice of the will. It's not motivated by feelings, because I sometimes feel like running up to my offender and ripping his lips off!

Trust

The test of *trust* is also important in knowing that my healing is complete. It's not that we have to trust the person who hurt us, but can we begin to trust people in general, and even to trust our own heart?

I was able to open my heart to my ex-husband, and we

remarried eight years after our divorce. Unfortunately, he relapsed and started his addictive behavior once again, and once again he was expelled from my home and my life. My heart still remains open to men, and I've gone on a few dates. I trust that God stands guard at the gate of my heart.

Another example was my relationship with my mother after all those years. During her last two years of life, I was able to open my heart to her by being a caring person to her. Eight weeks before she died and two weeks before I moved out of her home, she brought up the incident with the plate. No apology. She just brought it up with the reminder that it was my fault. We were sorting through some of her crystal and silver, and as I pulled out a platter, she engaged me in the following dialogue.

Mom said, "That's your plate."

"What plate?" I asked.

"The one I threw at you," she said without any emotion.

I said, "Oh, when I had to go to the emergency room and get stitches in my nose?"

Mom answered, "Yes, you wouldn't quit moving it."

I asked her, "How old was I, Mom?"

She said, "You were in kindergarten."

She handed me those sad facts with a calm tone, a cold heart, and a blank face. No remorse, and she seemed smug about the whole thing. I remained calm as I finished sorting through the rest of the crystal. I was grateful to God for his peace that day and for not letting me get hooked into an ugly argument. She was clueless of the pain she had caused me from that day of wounding, and I resigned to the fact that she would never value me as a person, much less a cherished child! She was sick and I am healed. Eight weeks after our conversation and with honor in my heart, I supervised her makeup and styled her hair one last time at the funeral home before her viewing. I could trust my heart to care for her then, and I could trust my heart to honor her at her funeral. Now Mom is forever healed and whole.

Hope

The third aspect of a true healing is being able to share our *testimony of hope*. The world needs to hear the testimony of a woman who is more than a conqueror. "More than" means *over and above the norm*. I am not a woman who is barely getting by in life's difficult experiences. I walk this planet with eternal life. I don't have to wait until I die to have eternal life—

I stepped into it the moment I asked God to be my Lord and Savior. He enables me to live over and above my common life here on earth. I don't just have life. I have a life that was raised from the dead! Inside my Bible cover are written these words:

Now my scars are my medals of commendations

My greatest direction came from my deepest rejection.

And these:

Thumbs down: My parents' rejection directed me toward a God who protects.

Thrown away: My husband's rejection directed me toward a God who is jealous for me.

Cancer: My health's rejection directed me toward a God who heals.

Turned down for credit: This economy's rejection directed me toward a God who provides.

For someone reading this book right now, the burden of suffering feels like a millstone hanging around your neck. But God wants you to see that in reality it is simply the weight necessary to hold a diver down while she searches for pearls!

My mom and me.

The very thing Satan uses to destroy you
can be the ministry on which God can build His kingdom.